The Idea *of* Leisure

The Idea of Leisure

First Principles

Robert A. Stebbins

Transaction Publishers
New Brunswick (U.S.A.) and London (U.K.)

Library of Congress Catalog Number: 2011023894
ISBN: 978-1-4128-4272-3
Printed in the United States of America

Library of Congress Cataloging-in-Publication Data

Stebbins, Robert A., 1938-
  The idea of leisure : first principles / Robert A. Stebbins.
      p. cm.
  Includes bibliographical references and index.
  ISBN 978-1-4128-4272-3
1. Leisure—Sociological aspects. I. Title.
  GV14.45.S82 2011
  306.4812—dc23
                    2011023894

To Jenna Hartel

Contents

List of Tables and Figures

Acknowledgments

Some of my ideas have longer gestation periods than others, and some I even have to induce to bring them into this world. The idea of leisure has been such for me; it has taken a long time to give birth to it, to beget for leisure studies a comprehensive definition of its central concept. I have thought for several years about the need for this definition, how I might develop it, and whether my colleagues in this field would welcome my efforts. But it took a lengthy conversation in a German restaurant with an Australian colleague working in Seoul to finally induce me, an American-Canadian, to get on with the intellectual parturition that is this book. Lawrence Bendle and I met just after the biannual congress of World Leisure in 2010, held near Seoul, to discuss our mutual passion for the study of leisure. He observed that the students, practitioners, and government officials he meets in and around Seoul, not to mention in Australia, typically find it most difficult to adequately grasp the nature of leisure. Moreover, he argued that, like the milieu of the restaurant, this is an international problem. If only all such people had a clear statement about what leisure is, their job would be so much easier. We toyed with numerous solutions to the problem. With plenty of time to consider the matter on the return flight to Canada, I conceived of the contents of this book.

The book, as general as it is and as anchored as it is in the serious leisure perspective (SLP), constitutes an appropriate occasion for acknowledging the fine work that Jenna Hartel has done for it through her publications and her service as webmaster of the SLP site. On a more practical plane, I am grateful for the usual, excellent editorial service provided by Transaction Publishers, this time that of Lawrence Mintz and Cheryl Lynn Eaton.

Introduction

The primary title of this book was inspired by the name of the international debate of the past two to three centuries that has swirled around "the idea of progress." Briefly put, it has been argued over this period by a range of thinkers in Western philosophy, religion, and the social sciences that, thanks to science, technology, and the organization of society, the human condition has improved and will continue to do so. They maintained that people are becoming progressively happier and enjoying an ever-improving quality of life, mostly because they are putting their skills and reason to work to reach positive ends of this sort.

But, as numerous critics of the idea of progress have also observed, if there has been progress, its manner of advancement is at best a sort of crab walk—slow and hesitant. And the most bitter among them see no real progress at all, as attested they say by such grisly examples as the twentieth-century descent into Nazism, genocide, and more recently, terrorism. Walter Moss (2008) and the *Economist* (December 17, 2009) have published punchy analyses, pro and con, of the idea of progress, suggesting that the notion remains current.

This book is based, in part, on the assumption that the idea of leisure can fit in this ferment as a singular but pivotal vector of progress, even though mention of leisure per se is extremely rare in the literature on the idea of progress. Be that as it may plenty of evidence exists (see the next paragraph and various sections of the present volume) for the proposition that leisure fosters positive development in both individual and community. True, progress through free-time activity may sometimes be difficult to glimpse, as observed in such deviant leisure as date rape, serial murder, and school-yard bullying. Nonetheless the vast majority of leisure activities often have profound, positive consequences for participants and society. Surely this can be conceived of as progress. In other words a good case can be made for linking leisure with progress.

1

This, then, is one broad intellectual debate in which this book may be framed. Yet the book is not primarily about leisure as progress, which is a matter of great complexity worthy of its own, necessarily large, volume. The present book is intentionally much shorter and much more rudimentary; it centers on essential first principles, on the unique properties of leisure which can be used to define it. The study of leisure lacks such a list, notwithstanding the essentialist-like essays of, for instance, Josef Pieper (1952) and Sebastian De Grazia (1964). In the following chapters, as a way of illuminating in abundant detail the very nature of leisure, I identify eight first principles. To be sure, doing this will help us understand how leisure is progressive (and how it sometimes is not). As I stated in *Personal Decisions in the Public Square: Beyond Problem Solving into a Positive Sociology* (published in 2009), leisure is the foundation of a positive personal and communal existence. And, apropos that book, I fear, in retrospect, that I have put the cart before the horse. To start, we need to understand fully what leisure is, before we can argue with clarity and conviction for its place in the march of progress.

So expect observations about the idea of leisure as part of the idea of progress to be sporadic, as we look in Chapter 1 at leisure and the individual, in Chapters 2 and 3 at the context of leisure as space and domain, and in Chapter 4 at the serious leisure perspective (SLP). It is only in Chapter 5 about leisure's image in the twenty-first century that the *idea* of leisure finally comes to center stage, and then only briefly. Still, as the reader moves through the extended discussion of first principles, he may want to remember that leisure does have huge import for all of humanity.

Thus it is no accident that the World Leisure Organization promotes the following motto: "Leisure: integral to social, cultural, and economic development." Nor is it an accident that Article 24 of the United Nations Universal Declaration of Human Rights is worded this way: "Everyone has the right to rest and leisure, including reasonable limitation of working hours and periodic holidays with pay." Leisure is important. For whole nations to find satisfaction and self-fulfillment based on it would be a true sign of progress. But, for that to happen, we need to first understand what leisure is. The following pages throw much needed light on this basic, but seriously ignored, requirement.

1

Leisure and the Individual

The goal of this book is to provide a detailed definition of leisure—what could be called a conceptual statement—that goes considerably beyond the definitions of the idea found in dictionaries, handbooks, key word compendia, and the like. Such definitions are intended to be short, which leaves them wanting in detail, however, for the books that contain them must also cover many other terms and concepts. This definitional practice, widespread as it is in the social sciences, leads at least in the case of the concept of leisure to misunderstandings. Crucial elements of a full definition are of necessity omitted in these attempts to produce a pithy, condensed statement.

Nevertheless, there are some important areas of contemporary life where condensed definitions are clearly inadequate. Here a much deeper understanding is required, as when politicians attempting to establish policy related to parks, tourism, recreation, or the amateur arts and sports need to know, for example, how participants in these areas are motivated, what problems they face, and how their leisure activities fit with the rest of society. Retirees unfamiliar with the vast world of leisure in which they now live can profit immensely from a detailed understanding of it. And, then, there are those happy souls whose work is so intrinsically attractive that it feels like leisure to them, leading some of them never to retire. A statement of this sort shows all these people the enormous range of leisure activities and their benefits to self and community. Such practitioners as clergy, physicians, and lifestyle counselors who occasionally face the need to discuss leisure with their followers, patients, and clients would also welcome a profound analysis of it.

I approach this detailed definition of leisure from two angles: leisure as seen and experienced by the individual participant and leisure as it fits in the wider social, cultural, and geographical world. As shorthand I refer to these as the *individual* and *contextual* approaches, and both are equally important in helping us define leisure. The present

3

chapter centers on the first, Chapter 2 on the second, and Chapter 3 on activity as an idea bridging the two approaches. Chapter 4 goes into still greater definitional depth, spanning further the two approaches by way of the SLP. Chapter 5 examines leisure's image and includes a sample of extensions into today's society of the detailed definition as developed over the course of the first four chapters.

The SLP forms, in the main, the theoretic foundation for the definitional work accomplished in this book. Among the general theories commonly discussed in leisure studies, the SLP is the only one whose origins lie substantially in research on free-time activity. That is the SLP emerged inductively from a foundational set of exploratory studies of various leisure activities (summarized in Stebbins 1992, 2001a, 2007a). For this reason the Perspective can be qualified as an *internal* theory and contrasted with the various *external* theories that have also been used to explain this sphere of life. Theories like functionalism, symbolic interactionism, critical analysis, and postmodernism contain some ideas on leisure, but they emerged in answer to intellectual questions quite distant from leisure. It follows that, when searching for the first principles with which to create a definition of leisure, whether detailed or condensed, it makes sense to look for them in this phenomenon's internal theory and research. Here is where we are most likely to find its essence, its unique features.

A Definition of Leisure

The condensed, dictionary-style definition of leisure used in this book is the following: *uncoerced, contextually framed activity engaged in during free time, which people want to do and, using their abilities and resources, actually do in either a satisfying or a fulfilling way (or both)* (modified from Stebbins [2005a], and subsequent publications). "Free time" in this book (it is further defined in Chapter 2) is time away from unpleasant, or disagreeable, obligation, with pleasant obligation being treated of here as essentially leisure. In other words *homo otiosus*, leisure man, feels no significant coercion to enact the activity in question (Stebbins 2000a). Some kinds of work—described in Chapter 4 as "devotee work"—can be conceived of as pleasant obligation, in that such workers though they must make a living performing their work, do this in a highly intrinsically appealing pursuit. Work of this sort is also essentially leisure, and will be regarded as such in this book. This definition is compatible with the SLP, particularly since the latter stresses human agency, or "intentionality" (Rojek 2010, 6)—what "people want to do"—and distinguishes the satisfaction gained from casual leisure vis-à-vis the fulfillment flowing from the serious form (see Chapter 4).

Note that reference to "free choice"—a long-standing component of standard definitions of leisure—is for reasons discussed more fully elsewhere (Stebbins 2005a), intentionally omitted from this definition. Generally put choice is never wholly free, but rather hedged about with all sorts of conditions. This situation renders this concept and allied ones such as freedom and state of mind useless as essential elements of a basic definition (Juniu and Henderson 2001). Note, too, that there is no reference in this definition to the moral basis of leisure as one of its distinguishing features; in other words, contrary to some stances taken in the past (e.g., Kaplan 1960, 22–25), leisure according to the SLP may be either deviant or nondeviant (see Chapter 4 of the present volume).

Uncoerced, people in leisure believe they are doing something they are not pushed to do, something they are not disagreeably obliged to do. In this definition, emphasis is ipso facto on the acting individual and the play of human agency. This in no way denies that there may be things people want to do but cannot do because of any number of constraints on choice, because of limiting social and personal conditions; for example, aptitude, ability, socialized leisure tastes, knowledge of available activities, and accessibility of activities. In other words, when using this definition of leisure, whose central ingredient is lack of coercion, we must be sure to understand leisure activities in relation to their larger personal, structural, cultural, and historical background, their context. And it follows that leisure is not really freely chosen, as some observers have claimed (e.g., Kelly 1990, 7; Parker 1983, 8–9), since choice of activity is significantly shaped by this background.

Nor may free time, as conventionally defined, be treated of here as synonymous with leisure. We can be bored in our free time, which can result from inactivity ("nothing to do") or from activity, which alas, is uninteresting, unstimulating. The same can, of course, happen at work and in obligated nonwork settings. Since boredom is a decidedly negative state of mind, it can be argued that, logically, it is not leisure at all. For leisure is typically conceived of as a positive mind set, composed of, among other sentiments, pleasant expectations and recollections of activities and situations. Of course, it happens at times that expectations turn out to be unrealistic, and we get bored (or perhaps angry, frightened, or embarrassed) with the activity in question, transforming it in our view into something quite other than leisure. And all this may happen in free time, which exemplifies well how such time can occupy a broader area of life than leisure, which is nested within it (Stebbins 2003).

Leisure as Activity

Our condensed definition refers to "uncoerced activity." An *activity* is a type of pursuit, wherein participants in it mentally or physically (often both) think or do something, motivated by the hope of achieving a desired end. Life is filled with activities, both pleasant and unpleasant: sleeping, mowing the lawn, taking the train to work, having a tooth filled, eating lunch, playing tennis matches, running a meeting, and on and on. Activities, as this list illustrates, may be categorized as work, leisure, or nonwork obligation. They are, furthermore, general. In some instances they refer to the behavioral side of recognizable roles, for example, commuter, tennis player, and chair of a meeting. In others we may recognize the activity but not conceive of it so formally as a role, exemplified in someone sleeping, mowing a lawn, or eating lunch (not as patron in a restaurant).

The concept of activity is an abstraction, and as such, one broader than that of role. In other words roles are associated with particular statuses, or positions, in society, whereas with activities, some are status based while others are not. For instance, sleeper is not a status, even if sleeping is an activity. It is likewise with lawn mower (person). Sociologists, anthropologists, and psychologists tend to see social relations in terms of roles, and as a result, overlook activities whether aligned with a role or not. Meanwhile, certain important parts of life consist of engaging in activities not recognized as roles. Where would many of us be could we not routinely sleep or eat lunch?

Moreover another dimension separates role and activity, namely, that of statics and dynamics. Roles are static whereas activities are dynamic.[1] Roles, classically conceived of, are relatively inactive expectations for behavior, whereas in activities, people are actually behaving, mentally or physically thinking or doing things to achieve certain ends. This dynamic quality provides a powerful explanatory link between an activity and a person's motivation to participate in it. Nevertheless, the idea of role *is* useful in positive sociology, since participants do encounter role expectations in certain activities (e.g., those in sport, work, volunteering). Although the concept of activity does not include

6

these expectations, in its dynamism, it can, much more effectively than role, account for invention and human agency.

This definition of activity gets further refined in the concept of *core activity*: a distinctive set of interrelated actions or steps that must be followed to achieve the outcome or product that the participant seeks. As with general activities core activities are pursued in work, leisure, and nonwork obligation. Consider some examples in serious leisure: a core activity of alpine skiing is descending snow-covered slopes, in cabinet making it is shaping and finishing wood, and in volunteer fire fighting is putting out blazes and rescuing people from them. In each case the participant takes several interrelated steps to successfully ski down hill, make a cabinet, or rescue someone. In casual leisure core activities, which are much less complex than in serious leisure, are exemplified in the actions required to hold sociable conversations with friends, savor beautiful scenery, and offer simple volunteer services (e.g., handing out leaflets, directing traffic in a theater parking lot, clearing snow off the neighborhood hockey rink). Work-related core activities are seen in, for instance, the actions of a surgeon during an operation or the improvisations on a melody by a jazz clarinetist. The core activity in mowing a lawn (nonwork obligation) is pushing or riding the mower. Executing an attractive core activity and its component steps and actions is a main feature drawing participants to the general activity encompassing it, because this core directly enables them to reach a cherished goal. It is the opposite for disagreeable core activities. In short, the core activity has motivational value of its own, even if more strongly held for some activities than others and even if some activities are disagreeable but still have to be done.

Core activities can be classified as simple or complex, the two concepts finding their place at opposite poles of a continuum. The location of a core activity on this continuum partially explains its appeal or lack thereof. Most casual leisure is comprised of a set of simple core activities. Here *homo otiosus* need only turn on the television set, observe the scenery, drink the glass of wine (no oenophile is he), or gossip about someone. Complexity in casual leisure increases slightly when playing a board game using dice, participating in a Hash House Harrier treasure hunt, or serving as a casual volunteer by, say, collecting bottles for the Scouts or making tea and coffee after a religious service. And Harrison's (2001) study of upper-middle-class Canadian mass tourists revealed a certain level of complexity in their sensual experience of the touristic sites they visited. For people craving the simple things in life, this is the kind of leisure to head for. The other two domains abound with equivalent simple core activities, as in the work of a parking lot attendant (receiving cash/making change) or the efforts of a householder whose nonwork obligation of the day is raking leaves.

So, if complexity is what people want, they must look elsewhere. Leisure projects are necessarily more complex than casual leisure activities. The types of projects listed in Chapter 4 provide, I believe, ample proof of that. Nonetheless, they are not nearly as complex as the core activities around which serious leisure revolves. The accumulated knowledge, skill, training, and experience of, for instance, the amateur trumpet player, hobbyist stamp collector, and volunteer emergency medical worker are vast, and defy full description of how they are applied during conduct of the core activity. Of course, neophytes in the serious leisure activities lack these acquisitions, though it is unquestionably their intention to acquire them to a level where they will feel fulfilled. As with simple core activities, complex equivalents also exist in the other two domains. Examples in work include the two earlier examples of the surgeon and jazz clarinetist. In the nonwork domain two common examples demonstrate a noticeable level of complexity: driving in city traffic and (for many people) preparing the annual income tax return.

Can all of life be characterized as an endless unfolding of activities? Probably not. For instance, the definition of activity does not fit things some people are, through violence, compelled to experience entirely against their will, including rape, torture, interrogation, forced feeding, and judicial execution. It would seem to be likewise for the actions of those driven by a compulsive mental disorder. There are also comparatively more benign situations in which most people still feel compelled to participate, among them, enduring receipt of a roadside traffic citation or a bawling out from the boss. Both fail to qualify as activities. In all these examples the ends sought are those of other people, as they pursue their activities. Meanwhile, the "victims" lack agency, unless they can manage to counterattack with an activity of resistance.

Activity as just defined is, by and large, a foreign idea in psychology, anthropology, and sociology. Sure, scholars there sometimes talk about, for instance, criminal, political, or economic activity, but in so doing, they are referring, in general terms, to a broad category of behavior, not a particular set of actions comprising a pursuit. Instead, our positive sociological concept of activity knows its greatest currency in the interdisciplinary fields of leisure studies and physical education and, more recently, kinesiology. And I suspect that the first adopted the idea from the second. There has always been, in physical education, discussion of and research on activities promoting conditioning, exercise, outdoor interests, human movement, and so on.

Leisure as Positive Activity

Positiveness is a personal sentiment felt by people who pursue those things in life they desire, the things they do to make their existence, rewarding, attractive, and therefore worth living (Seligman and Csikszentmihalyi 2000; Stebbins 2009a). Such people feel positive about these aspects of life. Because of this sentiment they may also feel positive toward life in general. A primary focus of positive social scientific research is on how, when, where, and why people pursue those things in life that they desire, on the things they do to create a worthwhile existence that, in combination, is substantially rewarding, satisfying, and fulfilling. General and core activities, sometimes joined with role, most of the time agreeable, but sometimes disagreeable, form the cornerstone of leisure. It is through certain activities that people, propelled by their own agency, find positive things in life, which they blend and balance with certain negative things they must also deal with. All this is carried out in the three previously mentioned domains.

The routes to the goal of positiveness are many. One is to strike a favorable work/leisure/obligation balance. The obligations referred to in this formula are those activities outside work we have to do, but in which we find little joy. Judith Nazareth (2007) writes at Generation Y, which was born between 1977 and 1999, will come closer than any of the preceding generations (Generation X, Baby Boomers) to the popular ideal of a decent work/leisure balance and, it follows, a more positive existence.

To a degree, this balance depends on a second route: finding one or more "formative careers." This is my label for a person's sense of continuous, positive self-development and self-fulfillment as it unfolds over the years in certain kinds of work and leisure. Fulfilling work and leisure—activity that expresses, often maximally, one's gifts and character—are most often found in the professions, consulting occupations, certain skilled trades, and certain small businesses. In leisure, fulfillment is experienced through the activities of amateurs, hobbyists, and skilled, knowledgeable volunteers.

Another route to positiveness is via attractive interpersonal relationships. Warm relations with close friends, relatives, and marital or live-in partners can add enormously to personal well-being in everyday life. The same may be said for a fourth route: positiveness that grows from being favorably involved in the community. The two principal vehicles for this are volunteering and the various kinds of collective leisure (e.g., playing a team sport, performing in a community orchestra, participating in a quilting club).

All these routes to positiveness are founded to a greater or lesser degree on leisure, our fifth route. As will be elaborated on shortly (Stebbins 2004a) even fulfilling work is essentially leisure; it just happens that some people make a living in such activity. Moreover, positive interpersonal relationships are always founded and maintained, in significant part, on a leisure base. But, alas, leisure does not invariably engender positiveness. The sorts of leisure just discussed will be described in Chapter 4 as "serious." They stand apart from activities qualified as "casual." The latter—it includes play, entertainment, sensory pleasures, relaxation, and social conversation—can be most helpful as, for example, in alleviating stress, establishing personal relationships, or simply allowing for a change of pace, all positive processes in life. Nevertheless, people can also overdo casual leisure to the point where it becomes deadening and therefore negative, evident in the all-too-common lament that "Life is dull, all I do is come home from a boring job and watch television."

The foregoing discussion of activity has been largely individual in approach. But activity is also contextualized, as will become evident in the next chapter. The same may be said for the experience of leisure.

Leisure as Experience

The experiential aspect of leisure is also evident in our short definition: "activity which people want to do and, in either a satisfying or a fulfilling way (or both)." The three basic forms of leisure set out in Chapter 4—casual, serious, and project-based—offer either satisfaction or fulfillment and, at times, both. Some of the forms, we will see later in this section, offer the experience of psychological flow as well.

Driver (2003, 168), who stresses the intrinsic nature of leisure behavior, holds that the leisure experience is a cardinal instance of it:

> Given that a human experience is a psychological or physiological response to encountering something, a leisure experience would be

any such response to a recreational engagement. All leisure experiences occur at the level of the individual, albeit strongly influenced by social and cultural contexts. Experiences can be psychological, physiological, or psycho-physiological in nature. As with humans leisure experiences have cognitive, affective, and connotative compounds.

People participating in leisure activities have as one main goal the desire for a satisfying or a fulfilling experience (Mannell 1999). Furthermore, they evaluate their involvement in these activities as good or bad, according to the level of satisfaction or fulfillment found there.

Flow, a form of optimal experience, is possibly the most widely discussed and studied generic intrinsic reward in the psychology of work and leisure. Although many types of work and leisure generate little or no flow for their participants, those that do are found primarily the "devotee occupations" (Stebbins 2004a) and serious leisure. Still, it appears that each work and leisure activity capable of producing flow does so in terms unique to it. And it follows that each activity must be carefully studied to discover the properties contributing to the distinctive flow experience it offers.

In his theory of optimal experience, Csikszentmihalyi (1990, 3–5, 54) describes and explains the psychological foundation of the many flow activities in work and leisure, as exemplified in chess, dancing, surgery, and rock climbing. Flow is "autotelic" experience, or the sensation that comes with the actual enacting of intrinsically rewarding activity. Over the years, Csikszentmihalyi (1990, 49–67) has identified and explored eight components of this experience. It is easy to see how this quality of complex core activity, when present, is sufficiently rewarding and, it follows, highly valued to endow it with many of the qualities of serious leisure, thereby rendering the two, at the motivational level, inseparable in several ways. And this even though most people tend to think of work and leisure as vastly different. The eight components are

1. sense of competence in executing the activity;
2. requirement of concentration;
3. clarity of goals of the activity;
4. immediate feedback from the activity;
5. sense of deep, focused involvement in the activity;
6. sense of control in completing the activity;
7. loss of self-consciousness during the activity;
8. sense of time is truncated during the activity.

These components are self-evident, except possibly for the first and the sixth. With reference to the first, flow fails to develop when the activity is either too easy or too difficult; to experience flow the participant must feel capable of performing a moderately challenging activity. The sixth component refers to the perceived degree of control the participant has over execution of the activity. This is not a matter of personal competence; rather it is one of degree of maneuverability in the fact of uncontrollable external forces, a condition well illustrated in situations faced by the mountain hobbyists mentioned above, as when the water level suddenly rises on the river or an unpredicted snowstorm results in a whiteout on a mountain snowboard slope.

Elkington (2010) has demonstrated that there is more to the flow experience than engaging in the core activities that generate it. His research subjects in table tennis, amateur theater, and voluntary sport coaching talked about the importance of their activities undertaken in preparation for experiencing flow and the importance of those undertaken afterward. He found that preflow preparation includes developing a feeling of being ready to participate in the activity and having a clear idea of what will be necessary to do this successfully. This includes developing trust with the other participants in the activity, so that, to the extent they are part of it, the individual will experience flow as expected. One common process observed in postflow was the participant's tendency to describe and analyze the earlier flow experience. The presence and absence of flow in serious, casual, and project-based leisure will be discussed in Chapter 4.

Leisure Today

The large majority of people in today's world covet their leisure time. Several of the reasons for doing so are obvious, as seen in the respite from work and the development of interpersonal relationships (including those in the family) made possible by participating in leisure activities. Moreover, certain kinds of leisure foster relaxation, while other kinds generate a sense of belonging to a valued group or social category. Yet, some of leisure's most profound benefits for the individual are the least obvious. We consider five here.

Leisure as the Precursor of Devotee Work

As just observed, working as an occupational devotee is very much like pursing serious leisure (Stebbins 2004a, chap. 5). Occupational devotion, which will be covered in greater depth in Chapter 4, refers to a strong, positive attachment to a form of self-enhancing work, where the senses of achievement and fulfillment are high and the core activity (set of tasks) is endowed with such intense appeal that the line between this work and leisure is virtually erased. An occupational devotee is someone inspired by occupational devotion. Devotee work is the core activity of the occupation. It is capable of inspiring occupational devotion.

Occupational devotees turn up chiefly, though not exclusively, in four areas of the economy, providing that the work there is, at most, only lightly bureaucratized: certain small businesses, the skilled trades, the consulting and counseling occupations, and the public- and client-centered professions. Public-centered professions are found in the arts, sports, scientific, and entertainment fields, while those that are client-centered abound in such fields as law, teaching, accounting, and medicine. Today's devotee occupations actually owe their existence in one way or another to one or more serious leisure precursors. Thus, some amateurs become professionals, some hobbyists become small business people, some volunteers become organizational employees.

So serious leisure and devotee work are much the same, even while the latter, in part because it is a livelihood, is obligated activity, albeit agreeably so. One crucial condition is that devotee work is fundamentally dependent on the domain of serious leisure. Bluntly put, without this leisure, the devotee occupations would never exist. This observation, when it comes to the trades and the client-centered professions, is apparent to most everyone, since they know of the preapprentice hobbyist and the preprofessional amateur. But when it comes to small businesses and the public-centered professions, it is, alas, sometimes overlooked. The student–amateur precursors of the former constitute a reasonably visible group, whereas the pure amateur–hobbyist–volunteer precursors of the latter are much less evident. With all the media hype surrounding professional athletes and entertainers, for instance, it is easy to forget that these people invariably come from a leisure background. Here they learned about their chosen field and their own taste and aptitude for it. Here is where their occupational devotion first took root. As for the student precursors, it should be noted that some may not be motivated by the amateur or hobbyist spirit, but rather by a sense of disagreeable obligation (e.g., "my parents insist that I become a lawyer," laments a student who would rather seek a career in music).

Leisure as an Avenue for Self-Development

Leisure and devotee work can be main sources of self-development and, especially, of self-fulfillment. The latter refers to the act or the process of developing to the full one's capacity, more particularly, developing one's gifts and character. Both unfold within the framework of a formative career (defined earlier). It is a subjective concept, two major components of which are the leisure career and that of devotee work. Of these two the first is the more foundational, since as just pointed out, today's devotee occupations actually owe their existence, in one way or another, to one or more serious leisure precursors.

A leisure career is the typical course, or passage, of a type of amateur, hobbyist, or volunteer that carries the person into and through a leisure role or activity and possibly into and through a work role (Stebbins 2007a, 18–22). The effect of human agency in a person's career in serious leisure (and possibly later in devotee work) is evident in his or her acquisition and expression of a combination of the special skills, knowledge, and experience associated with the core activities. Furthermore, every serious leisure career both frames and is framed by the continuous search for certain rewards, a search that takes months, and in some fields years, before the participant consistently finds deep fulfillment in the chosen amateur, hobbyist, or volunteer role or sometimes later on, in a variety of devotee work (these rewards are discussed in Stebbins [2007a, 13–17]). The leisure career, thus understood, is, it should now be clear, a major source of motivation to continue pursuing the leisure or devotee work activity.

Leisure as a Source of Personal and Social Identity

Serious leisure participants tend to identify strongly with their chosen pursuits. No small wonder. With their formative careers it is inevitable that they would come to see themselves, usually proudly, as a certain kind of amateur, hobbyist, or career volunteer. True, self-perception as a particular kind of amateur depends on how far into the career the individual has got. Neophytes—serious leisure participants at the beginning of their formative career but intending to stay with the activity and develop in it—are unlikely to identify themselves as true amateurs or hobbyists. To do that, they must believe they are good enough at it to stand out from its dabblers, even while they are comparatively weak vis-à-vis more experienced participants, including in the case of amateurs, the professionals in their field.

Identity has both a social and a psychological side. Thus, a person's identity is part of his personality, which in one sense, is a psychological matter. The individual enthusiast's view of self as an ongoing participant in complex leisure activity (serious and project-based forms) is a situated expression of this personal identity. It is based on dimensions like level of skill, knowledge, and experience as well as number and quality of physical acquisitions (e.g., good health, collectibles) and lasting physical products (quilts, paintings) stemming from the leisure. So, a young woman might remark to a new acquaintance that she is a skateboarder, but qualify the image she is projecting by indicating that she has only been in the hobby for two years. She is a skateboarder and proud of it, but do not look to her, at least just yet, for expert demonstrations of its core activities. This presentation of self to the acquaintance is a sociological matter, however, in that the skateboarder not only wants the other to know about her leisure but also for that person to form an accurate impression of her ability to partake in it.

A person's social identity refers to the collective view that the other people in a particular leisure setting hold of these same levels and acquisitions. It is by social identity, among other ways, that the community (including family, neighbors, friends) places people in social space. So, John not only sees and identifies himself as a coin collector, but also various members of the community identify him this way. The fact that complex leisure offers a distinctive personal and social identity is central to personal development. Moreover, it is a point that leisure educators should emphasize. For such an identity is unavailable in casual leisure—the leisure most people know—suggesting therefore that the large majority of people receiving leisure education will find the idea a novelty.

Leisure can Lead to High Quality of Life and Well-Being

High quality of life, however generated, is a state of mind, which to the extent people are concerned with their own well-being, must be pursued with notable diligence. (Did we not speak earlier of career and agency?) Moreover, high quality of life does not commonly "fall into one's lap," as it were, but roots in desire, planning, and patience, as well as a capacity to seek deep satisfaction through experimentation with all three forms of leisure to eventually carve out an optimal leisure and work lifestyle. In other words, human agency is the watchword here.

Leisure/lifestyle counselors in psychology can advise and inform about a multitude of leisure activities that hold strong potential for elevating quality of life, but, in the end, it is the individual who must be motivated to pursue them and stick to a plan (possibly generated in collaboration with a counselor) for doing this. And leisure policy can be developed such that people have opportunities to find a high quality of life. Furthermore, the drive to find this level of living helps explain the purchases some people make to facilitate pursuing a serious or casual leisure activity.

What then of well-being? For this book I privilege the social variety, as opposed to its subjective counterpart. Keyes (1998, 121) defines social well-being as the "absence of negative conditions and feelings, the result of adjustment and adaptation to a hazardous world." For him well-being, though a personal state, is influenced by many of the social conditions considered earlier or considered in Chapter 4 as part of the SLP. Though the relationship is probably more complex than this, for purposes of the present discussion, let us incorporate in the following proposition what has been said to this point in this section: social well-being emanates from a high quality of life, as generated by serious leisure or devotee work or both, with either of or both of these being rounded out some casual or project-based leisure (or both).

Leisure as the Basis for a Positive Lifestyle

Every period of history has experienced negativeness, as manifested in the upsetting problems of the day that people want solved. Meanwhile, a number of contemporary problems—some of the most celebrated being terrorism, genocide, global warming, and extraordinary economic decline—seem intractable and negative to the extreme. Yet, in many parts of the world, where its inhabitants are not directly affected by such worries (e.g., the rest of India and even greater Mumbai during terrorism in that city in November 2008), life in its daily round goes on more or less as usual.

How is it possible to adapt to such negativeness when it poses a vague but nonetheless omnipresent threat? A main answer is that people still manage to find positive features in their lives, features to which they give priority. With this orientation they work out a positive lifestyle, founded for most of them on their free-time resources. These features make life worthwhile, a condition that, even if all problems were solved, could never be achieved. Why, because positiveness is much more than an absence of negativeness, even though such absence would help focus attention on the first.

The basic social sciences are dominantly concerned with either solving problems or describing them. In this sense they are far more interested in negativeness and description than in positiveness. Leisure studies, whose subject matter is inherently positive, can show the basic social sciences why they should also care about positiveness and its roots in leisure.

Conclusion

This brings us to the end of our explication of the individual approach to defining leisure, leisure as the experience of positive activity. Rather little has been said about the contextual element in the condensed definition set out near the beginning of this chapter, the social and cultural arrangements that frame activity engaged in during free time. The next three chapters help correct, each in its own way, this conceptual imbalance. There it is observed, for instance, that leisure is also a social institution with its own geographic roots. It is perhaps relatively easy to see leisure from the individual angle taken in the present chapter, because this view taps directly into our experience of it. Seeing leisure contextually requires a capacity to view social life more abstractly, beyond one's own immediate free-time involvements in it. Be that as it may a full understanding of leisure—a full definition of it—requires nothing less than also seeing it in sociocultural–geographic context.

But, first, having now had a look at some of the essential features of leisure as a phenomenon and therefore as a concept, do they appear to add up to something that is, in combination, unique? The field of leisure studies seems to think such a conception is impossible. Chris Rojek (2010, 99) writes:

> From the start, the academic study of leisure has been dogged by the question of what theoretical and methodological tools have been custom-built and what is borrowed or rebranded from the larger established and more powerful Social Sciences. Within the field of Leisure Studies there is a discernible reluctance to claim innovation or novelty.

He goes on to cite John Kelly and Ken Roberts, two prominent scholars in leisure studies, as arguing that their central subject—leisure—defies unique definition, is not uniquely distinctive.[2] Hence,

17

they conclude, the best road for leisure studies to follow is through interdisciplinary links, which of course, steers attention away from trying to isolate leisure's essential properties and to formulate a definition based on them.

Be that as it may we have in this chapter already identified some unique, essential principles of leisure that distinguish it from other phenomenon, gained in part by widening the scope of leisure to include devotee work. They are: (1) leisure is uncoerced (general) activity; (2) leisure is core activity that participants want to do; and (3) leisure is pursued in free time, defined as time away from disagreeable obligation. No other human phenomenon may be characterized by any one of these properties or by any two or three of them in combination. This is the first statement in this book about the unique features of leisure; they are truly first principles. Specifically, in the coming chapters, I will add five more unique principles to these three.

Notes

1. I am aware that general sociological theory conceives of roles as dynamic and statuses as static. Compared with activities, however, roles are *relatively* static.
2. Rojek, by the way, does not seem to accept this evaluation of the field of leisure studies, but merely reports on it in his discussion of its history and present-day situation.

2

Leisure in Context

In this chapter we turn to leisure's context. In particular, we will consider the three spaces of leisure: institutional, temporal, and geographical. When leisure is conceived of as space, we at once describe and define it from this perspective. That is leisure may be defined and examined as it fits in the culture and social organization of community and society, as it fits in the span of daily, weekly, and yearly time, and as it fits in the surrounding environment, whether artificial or natural. Analyses of leisure often proceed from two or, at times, all three of these definitions, but to underscore their distinctive features, they will be treated of separately here.

Institutional Space

When leisure is conceived of as an institution (e.g., Kaplan 1975, 28–31; Rojek 2000), the thought immediately evokes a tendency to see it in relation to the other institutions of society. That is by noting that leisure is an institution is to say that it is not, for example, family, economy, polity, education, religion, health, or the arts. The institution of leisure intersects in diverse ways with all these institutions, and others not mentioned, but is nonetheless its own structural/cultural entity.

A standard sociological definition of a social institution is that it is a relative stable set of abstract relationships, patterns of behavior, roles, norms, and values that emerge as solutions to a set of problems associated with a certain sphere of collective living. The collective problem around which leisure has institutionalized is that of how, according to its norms and values, people in a society use their free time effectively and acceptably. Institutions solve, albeit not always ideally according to all the people involved, the problems they want solved such that they can get through a normal year.

There exist numerous patterns of leisure behavior and motivation associated with particular leisure activities as pursued by different segments of the population. These activities include stamp collecting, playing chess, watching television, going to the movies, and attending cocktail parties. Baseball games, electronic games, the amateur theater, the racetrack, the ski slopes—all part of leisure. There are also many abstract relationships within leisure, as exemplified in the relationship between amateur actors and the director of a theater company. At the group level, there are relationships among clubs, associations, centers, and the like. Furthermore, leisure roles are in evidence everywhere (in theaters, in hockey arenas, on trout streams, on ski slopes, over chessboards, in front of television sets). Three of the main values of leisure are the desire for pleasure (hedonism), the desire for variety in the experiences from which pleasure is derived, and the desire to choose one's leisure.

So far I have described what the institution of leisure contains, established roles, activities, values, and so on. Beyond this edifice lies the fact that all institutions also constrain the behavior of people living within them. This is context. The institution for these people tends to channel their choices of activities, role, values, and the like by dint of being the most visible and by being acceptable. Rojek (2010, chap. 3) offers several detailed examples of the way social institutions frame leisure behavior. He also shows in later chapters how the state and corporations accomplish the same thing. In doing this they too contribute, often in ways too complicated and subtle to be pursued in this book, to the structure and culture of the leisure institution. Yet, in his final chapter he holds, as I do in this book, that leisure abounds within this framework, and that people occasionally, if not often, flout it by taking up deviant leisure and new leisure (considered in Chapter 3, see also Stebbins [2009c]). In other words there is, in all this, plenty of scope for human agency, for what people "want to do."

Leisure in the Economy

Leisure turns up in certain institutions outside the leisure institution itself, although its appearance there is, as it were, fleeting. Thus, in traditional economics and the mainstream economics of today, the idea of leisure is typically residual (Oberg 2008). Accordingly, the few definitions of leisure that appear in the dictionaries of economics are superficial, largely portraying leisure as time leftover after work. For example, Weiss (2009, 3) asks the question: how we may distinguish leisure from work? He quotes W. S. Jevons (2006, 168) who defines labor as "any painful exertion of mind or body undergone partly or wholly with a view to future good." Weiss goes on to observe that

> applying the (newly discovered) principle of diminishing marginal utility (and increasing marginal disutility), Jevons shifted attention from work or leisure as such to the marginal units of each activity. A person stops working only when the marginal disutility of work exceeds the marginal utility of the consumption derived from additional work, which is presumed positive when the wage is positive.

Later, Weiss draws on Gary Becker (1965, 504). The latter concludes that "although the social philosopher might have to define precisely the concept of leisure, the economist can reach all his traditional results, as well as many more, without introducing it at all!"

Despite this stance, Bruno Frey (2008) devotes an entire chapter to procedural utility and happiness. He defines this utility as "the well-being gained from living and acting under institutionalized processes that also contribute to a positive sense of self and address the innate needs for autonomy, relatedness, and competence." Although Frey never uses the term leisure, this statement about happiness, in general, may be interpreted as also related to leisure, in particular. He shows, inadvertently, how a detailed understanding of the idea of leisure can enrich economic analysis. Further might not the study of the economics of health be enriched by observations in leisure studies that some leisure activities exercise the brain better than others (e.g., playing chess or pursuing a liberal arts reading hobby vis-à-vis watching television or drinking at the pub)? Or what about consumption, often considered in economics under the heading of "household behavior and family economics"? The author (Stebbins 2009b) argues, for example, that consumption for casual leisure differs from that for serious leisure, in that, for the latter, participants often purchase goods and services to facilitate self-fulfillment as gained through the activity. A full explanation of consumption for leisure must incorporate this proposition.

Leisure in the Polity

Political science appears not to include in its core conceptual framework the concept of leisure, whether its own or one imported from leisure studies. Leisure appears in none of its dictionaries. Still the concept has occasionally entered into recent analyses in political science. Thus, Davies and Niemann (2002, 572–73), upon examining the relationship of leisure and international relations, found that it is during free time in everyday life when the vast majority of people can take an interest in world affairs. This they do by reading the newspaper, watching television, reading novels or going to the cinema, doing what may be classified as casual leisure for most participants. It is through such uncoerced activities that the general, not-professionally trained public has access to what is happening in international relations.

Possibly the best known link between leisure and political science is found in the voluminous literature on political participation. This process has been defined as individual political voluntary action intended to affect governmental social policy, policy implementation, and decision making, whether at a local (i.e., citizen participation), regional, national, or international level. Political participation ranges from voting to involvement in political nonprofit groups. It may be motivated by selfish or altruistic goals, sometimes both. However motivated, it is voluntary behavior and as such a kind of leisure. Note, however, that the nature of political participation will vary by whether the leisure sought in it is serious, casual, or project-based. For instance a political scientist would surely want to know when quantitative measures of such participation are largely evanescent, as in voting (say, as casual or project-based activity), and largely enduring, as in working on party policy or recruiting electoral candidates (serious leisure). Sydney Verba's work (e.g., Verba, Nie, and Kim 1978) stands out in this area as does that of Rosenstone and Hansen (1993).

There is also the political process of allocating leisure resources. This is a matter of policy at all levels of government concerned with supplying such leisure amenities as parks, recreational centers, and athletic facilities. It is common for people employed in these establishments to be trained in leisure studies, enabling them to apply existing knowledge about types of leisure, motivation to pursue them, requirements for satisfying and fulfilling leisure experiences, and the positive consequences of such experiences for personal and communal health.

There are two other angles from which to view leisure in institutional space. One is through leisure in historical perspective and through leisure as a distinctive domain of activities. The second angle is covered in Chapter 3. In the present chapter we first examine the historical evolution of leisure as related to work and then consider the history of leisure activity. Leisure, being as old as the human species, was present at the start of its history.

Evolution of the Leisure–Work Relationship

Thus, there was surely leisure in the early subsistence societies, even though empirical evidence of this claim is scarce. Viewed from the standpoint of work and leisure, much of the history of mankind has been about subsistence as a livelihood, with free-time activity taking place in the comparatively few hours left over after seeing to life's basic needs. Hunting, fishing, and gathering food; raising and harvesting crops; and moving to new land that facilitates all of these, along with defending against enemies, human and animal, occupy a lot of time in a preindustrial society. But life on this subsistence level must necessarily include a few hours off for games, dancing, music, relaxation, sexual activity, casual conversation, and the like.

Hamilton-Smith (2003, 225–26) writes that archaeological findings on this sort of leisure gathered from artifacts, living sites, cave painting, and so on, dates as far back as the prehistoric cultures. McBrearty and Stringer (2007) write that

> all humans today express their social status and group identity through visual clues such as clothing, jewelry, cosmetics and hairstyle. Shell beads, and haematite used as pigment, show that this behaviour dates to 80,000 years ago in coastal North and South Africa...Ochre seems to have been a material with both symbolic and utilitarian functions. The colour red is fundamental to colour classifications in all known human societies, and it seems probable that the substance was indeed used for body painting and to colour artefacts by 165,000 years ago. (764)

Since there seems to be no evidence on the matter, we may only speculate that some disagreeable nonwork obligations (discussed in Chapter 3) also troubled subsistence peoples, whatever the time in history during which they lived. Some of these may have been religious, exemplified in carrying out animal and human sacrifices and participating in sacred rituals. Perhaps there was also the occasional need for mediating family differences, in addition to engaging in activities intended to uphold honor and mete out justice to those felt to have violated group rules. Further it is conceivable that, in their own way, these societies ministered to their sick and injured, arranging for customary disposal of the dead when these actions failed.

In this discussion of work, leisure, and obligation in subsistence times, I have used these concepts as defined in this book. Still it is doubtful that people living then were oriented by these ideas.

Nevertheless, they did believe in what they had to do to survive in their world, however scientifically accurate this knowledge. Furthermore, the activities implementing the knowledge were not seen as optional. Today we call this work. Additionally there were activities that would seem to be optional as well as enjoyable, including relaxing, dancing, making and listening to music, and at least some of the time, sexual relations. In modern times this is leisure. But what about obligations? I suspect that, though they must have existed then, they were probably poorly understood, or understood simply as customary activities people are supposed to engage in. In this regard little has changed, for the modern commonsense understanding of the idea is, at bottom, only marginally more advanced.

Furthermore, work and leisure, however understood, were probably in these societies also sometimes difficult to distinguish. If the hunt is a fulfilling work activity (consisting of, for instance, skill in tracking, knowledge of animal habits, developed prowess with bow or spear), whatever the basic need it fills, is it not akin to the occupational devotion of the modern age? Is not decorating a clay pot, which with this activity pushes it beyond its utilitarian value as a receptacle for water, also an expression of an acquired artistic skill? Again, does this not resemble devotee work? In short, occupational devotion may be far older than suggested in the preceding chapter.

Western Societies

Sylvester (1999, 18–23) writes that, from classical antiquity through the Middle Ages, two streams of thought influenced modern-day Western beliefs about and attitudes toward work and leisure. One had its roots in Ancient Greece, especially in the city-state of Athens, while the other emerged later in the ferment of early Christianity.

Classical Greece

The actual patterns of work and leisure among ordinary people during this period, it appears, were quite different from what its "gentlemen-philosophers"—most notably Plato and Aristotle—had to say about them (Sylvester 1999, 18). These intellectuals were unusual people in Greek society, for they had sufficient free time during which they could philosophize about these two domains and their relationship. We will concentrate in this section on some of the key ideas of the two men, primarily because those ideas have had considerable impact on Western thought on work and leisure and because the historical record of these domains in the rest of ancient Greek society is inadequate.

Plato argued that leisure was a necessary condition for anyone devoting himself to the activity of discovering truth (use of masculine gender is intentional here, for females were not considered part of this class). The thinker engaged in this pursuit had to be free from the demands of securing a livelihood. As for the discovery of truth, this was strictly the province of intellectuals of superior breeding. In particular, these intellectuals were philosophers; they were the only people capable of discovering truth, or "knowledge," while also providing civic leadership. The truth in question, by the way, was not knowledge based on sensory experience (sight, taste, touch, etc.), subject to change in light of new empirical evidence—scientific knowledge—but rather knowledge in the unchangeable, transcendental shape of ideas, or "forms"—philosophical knowledge.

In this system, the common man, who was sometimes a slave, labored for his own livelihood as well as that of the gentlemen-philosophers. Such was his lot in life. Work is honored here because it supports someone else's freedom from work and that person's pursuit of excellence in the creation of knowledge. Of course, the ordinary worker gained little more from all this than his livelihood.

Aristotle wrote about what has been translated into English as the "good life." Integral to this life, he said, is achieving excellence in morality and intellectual pursuits. Moral excellence, he argued, comes with contemplating how best to live both individually and socially, whereas intellectual excellence grows from understanding and delighting in the true principles of the universe. Also included in the good life is engaging in such activities as speech (oratory), music, friendship, gymnastics, and citizenship. Moreover, according to Sylvester (1999, 20), Aristotle viewed work as "severely encroaching on the good life. Only when people were liberated from having to work for the necessities of life could they turn to the good life." It follows that leisure, which in ancient Greece was freedom from having to work, is itself a condition of the good life. Consistent with this line of reasoning was Aristotle's assertion that happiness also depends on leisure.

A citizen, or a person holding citizenship in a Greek city-state, also enjoyed leisure. Yet, as such, he was no laborer. Furthermore, citizens were expected to keep themselves geographically apart from the rest, from noncitizens. The former even had their special agora, in which leisure on the order of the activities listed in the preceding paragraph was pursued. By contrast, the agora of the latter was a place for trade, a commercial arena for facilitating the exchange of things the working class made or grew.

Notwithstanding their self-serving model of society, neither Plato nor Aristotle viewed work as inherently demeaning. Rather what was demeaning was the requirement that a person labor, for this created a dependence on work. In other words, if ordinary people fail to work, they will gain no livelihood and therefore soon perish. Additionally, the two philosophers maintained it is demeaning to be unable to experience happiness and realize excellence, both being achievable only during leisure.

Sylvester (1999, 21–23) qualifies the foregoing as an elitist conception of work and leisure in ancient Greece, noting further that, unfortunately, it is the only recorded statement on leisure available for that era. He explained that: "by applying higher and more rigorous standards to the concept of freedom, aristocrats were able to underscore their superiority while defining the *demos* [common people] as unfree, licentious, and unworthy. Furthermore, aristocrats identified *freedom* from labor, a condition synonymous with leisure, as a vital form of freedom" (22). As the aristocrats viewed the world the narrow training of the craftsman rendered him unfit for leisure. By contrast, aristocratic training consisted of education in the liberal arts of music, philosophy, speech, and the like. Aristocratic excellence was further expressed in war, sport, and competitions in music, among other pursuits, all of which could be defined today as serious leisure.

Nonetheless, what little evidence there is suggests that the *demos* clearly took pride in their craft work. But it also appears that they failed to value work for its own sake; as a general activity it was never glorified. In the language of this book, the *demos*, when its workers could find self-fulfillment in their labor, did certainly value its core activities and the products they created through their efforts. These craftsmen were independent workers, much like, we might say, some of the small business crafts people of today, described earlier as occupational devotees.

The Judeo-Christian Era

During the Judeo-Christian period, work came to be glorified, particularly as an avenue leading to spiritual development. Beside its necessity as a livelihood, work was thought to foster desirable habits, among them, sobriety, discipline, and industry. Furthermore, work engendered a certain independence in the worker and, apparently (Sylvester 1999, 24), a sense of charity. Unlike in the days of ancient Greece, work in the Judeo-Christian tradition was ultimately held to be undertaken for the glory of God as well as to instill a level of sacredness in those who worked here on Earth.

In the Middle Ages, Christian monasticism revolved around work, through which the monks in retreat in monasteries sought religious purity in manual labor and the reading of divine literature. Leisure, in this situation, was held in low regard. It took St. Thomas Aquinas to restore it to the dignified position it enjoyed in ancient Greece. Aquinas argued that, if a man could live without labor, he was under no obligation to engage in it. Indeed, spiritual work was only possible when the thinker was freed of physical labor. The elevated place of the contemplative life was thus restored, and with it the value of leisure.

With the advent of the Renaissance, the balance of prestige between work and leisure shifted somewhat. This was a period of creative activity, which rested substantially on practical achievements in art and craft. Experimental physical science also took root during this era, initially as a (serious) leisure pursuit. Nevertheless, the skilled artist, craftsman, and scientist were, themselves, special people. Ordinary manual laborers were still regarded as lowly by this group and the rest of the elite, thereby enabling these higher ranks in society to retain their superiority, backed by leisure as one of the differentiating principles.

The Protestant Reformation

Al Gini (2001, 20–21) has observed that, together, the Renaissance and the Protestant Reformation have served as a cardinal reference point in the development of the modern work ethic. He points out that "it was during this period that work, no matter how high or low the actual task, began to develop a positive ethos of its own, at least at the theoretical level" (20). More particularly, Sylvester (1999, 26) writes: "the Protestant work ethic was one of the central intellectual developments in changing attitudes toward labor and leisure. In it work is more than a livelihood, it is also a man's raison d'être."

The Protestant ethic, seldom mentioned today in lay circles and possibly not much discussed there even during its highest point in the seventeenth and eighteenth centuries, has nevertheless been a prominent social force in the evolution of Western society. Culturally and structurally, this powerful personal orientation motivating the small-enterprise capitalists of the day left its mark, one so powerful that it is still being felt in the present. This is because the Protestant ethic is, at bottom, about the will to work.

Max Weber and the Protestant Ethic

Max Weber published, in German in 1904, the first section of his essay "The Protestant Ethic and the Spirit of Capitalism," shortly before he set out to visit the United States. Upon returning at the end of 1904 to his native Germany, he published (in 1905) the second part, which was much informed by his observations on American society and its capitalist economic system. Following Weber's death in 1920 the essay was reprinted, along with a number of lengthier works, in one of several large volumes released in the early 1920s. Not long thereafter, Talcott Parsons translated and published as a small book, with direct translation of the title, the only English edition of "The Protestant Ethic..." (Weber 1930).

Gerth and Mills (1958, 25) said of Weber that "although he was personally irreligious—in his own words, 'religiously unmusical'—he nevertheless spent a good part of his scholarly energy in tracing the effects of religion upon human conduct and life." Weber's treatise on the Protestant ethic and the spirit of capitalism—his most celebrated essay—is, among other things, about individual men (women are never mentioned in the essay) becoming motivated to pursue the value of success and achievement in an occupation defined by each as a divine calling. It is also about how Western capitalism as an economic system (as opposed to great individual undertakings) evolved in part from the activities of these men. Weber was interested in the worldly asceticism of seventeenth- and eighteenth-century Protestantism, of which Calvinism was the purest instance. In particular, he was concerned with Calvin's principle of predestination. Calvin had argued that only a small proportion of all people are chosen for grace, or eternal salvation, whereas the rest are not. This arrangement cannot be changed, for it is God's will.

But, alas, the chosen do not know they have been chosen. The tension of not knowing whether you number among the elect could nevertheless be assuaged in this world by maintaining an implicit trust in Christ, the result of true faith. Moreover, it is a man's duty to consider himself chosen and to act as though this were true, evidence for which came from avoiding worldly temptations like sloth and the hedonic pleasures and from treating work as a calling. A calling—a task set by God but nonetheless chosen by mortals—refers as well to a man's duty to enact his occupational role to the best of his abilities, using his personal powers or material possessions and abstaining from creature pleasures and other leisure activities. This was measured, in part, by usefulness for the community of the goods produced in it. But the most important criterion was found in the realm of capitalist enterprise: amassing wealth through thrift, profit, diligence, investments, sobriety, and similar virtues, and not doing this as an end in-itself. Success and achievement in an occupation, whatever their nature, generate self-confidence, thereby reinforcing a man's belief that he has been chosen. In other words, God helps those who help themselves.

While acknowledging in passing that there were others, Weber concentrated primarily on "callings" or "professions" (referred to in this book in modern terms as "occupations") that made it possible to amass wealth. Achieving significant wealth helped generate self-confidence. Hard work, savings, investment, and shrewd decisions in commercial activities all constituted evidence of a man's belief in his own eternal salvation. The result was the emergence of a new social class of self-made entrepreneurs and soon thereafter their integration into the system of Western capitalism as we know it in the present. Weber's object of study was the men who established the family-firm type of capitalist business, common in Western Europe and the United States from the seventeenth century to the present.

According to Cohen (2002, 5), Weber was unclear about the relation-ship between modern capitalist institutions and the Puritans' spirit of capitalism. Still, from his extensive examination of historical evidence, Cohen (2002, 254) was able to conclude that "English Puritanism aided capitalism, but its impact was weaker and less dramatic than Weber claimed." Moreover, the impact, attenuated as it was, was primarily cultural, in that helped legitimate further the emerging capitalism of the day and helped mold the broader work ethic as it was taking shape at that time in Occidental culture.

The Protestant Ethic Today

The Protestant ethic, as a summary concept for a distinctive set of motives to work, is largely a dead letter today (it was already in serious decline even at the time Weber wrote about it), though some people still work long hours in pursuit of a variety of more worldly rewards. David Riesman and others (1961) argued that the inner-directed men of the 1950s, who were oriented by the Protestant ethic, were being rapidly replaced by other-directed men whose love of mass culture was their singular trait. Otherworldly in orientation as it was, the Protestant ethic, it appears, was nevertheless an important cultural precursor of the modern work ethic. It helped steer the search for the cultural value of activity toward the domain of work (as opposed to that of leisure); work is good and hard work is still better.

Although the Protestant ethic was, in fact, both a cultural and an individual phenomenon, Weber wrote mostly about its psychological side; he looked on the ascetic Protestants as constituting a distinctive type of personality with its own worldview. Analysis of the Protestant ethic as a personal worldview reveals three central components. One is attitude: a person should work, work hard, and avoid leisure as much as possible. The second is value: work activity is good, whereas leisure activity is not. The third component is belief: by hard work people can demonstrate their faith that they number among the chosen. On the macroanalytic level, we find in societies where the Protestant ethic is widely shared that all three personal components are also widely shared. Thus, the Protestant ethic is also part of the culture of these societies. And speaking of culture, the Protestant ethic, as mentioned already, also contributed significantly to the rise of the economic system that came to be known as capitalism. That system is now a main social institution in modern Western society.

Another reason for the decline of the Protestant ethic is that it never could become the guiding orientation for all paid work, including certain kinds that were carried out even during the heyday of the ethic (Stebbins 2004a, 26–27). True, Weber wrote, albeit briefly, about all callings and the requirement that those pursuing them demonstrate through hard work their chosen place in Heaven. But then he went on to concentrate exclusively on the capitalist trades and the accumulation of wealth in that sphere. Perhaps, for Weber, the problem was that many other occupations fail to produce evidence of diligence so tangible, countable, and incontrovertible as property and monetary riches. As a result, in Weber's day, as in modern times, there were and still are numerous occupations that, at bottom, lie outside the purview of his essay, including those requiring altruistic service to humankind (e.g., nursing, teaching) and extensive development of personal skills and knowledge (e.g., science, sport, the arts).

It is quite possible therefore that, at the time when the Protestant ethic was a prominent motive for many workers, others were enamored instead of occupations with great intrinsic appeal, but which could offer as evidence of having been chosen few convincing ways of publicly displaying diligence and excellence. Put otherwise, these latter occupations were intrinsically attractive, a quality found in the enactment of the work itself rather than in extrinsic rewards it produced such as high remuneration and great profit. It was, in general, difficult to measure, simply and publicly, intrinsic rewards, such that they could constitute proof of the worker's place among the elect. In brief, occupational devotion lay beyond the scope of Weber's essay.

These intrinsically fulfilling occupations, which were in effect beyond the purview of the Protestant ethic, grew in importance during the twentieth century. And the modern "work ethic," being broader than its religious cousin, the Protestant ethic, finds expression in them as well. What, then, is the work ethic, the ethic that dominates in modern times?

The Work Ethic and its Variants

By mid-twentieth century the salvation component of the Protestant ethic can be observed, as already noted, only in the outlook of David Riesman's (Riesman et al. 1961) inner-directed man, who by then, was nevertheless a vanishing breed. What was left by that point in history of the West's distinctive orientation toward work has been known all along simply as the "work ethic." This more diffuse ethic, in fact, shares two of the three components of the Protestant version mentioned earlier. It shares the same attitudes: a person should work, work hard, and avoid leisure as much as possible. It also shares the same values: work is good, while leisure is not. Only the third component is missing—that of belief: by hard work people can demonstrate their faith that they number among the chosen. In short, the work ethic is but a secular version of the Protestant ethic.

One widely discussed characteristic of today's work ethic has been described as "workaholism," an orientation that has probably been around as long as the work ethic itself and that may be seen as another offshoot of the Protestant ethic. Marilyn Machlowitz (1980) pioneered this concept, in an attempt to help explain why a conspicuous minority of modern workers, though not guided by the Protestant ethic, are still exceptionally drawn to their work. Part of this attraction is positive, she said; they find in their work many intrinsic rewards. The other part, however, is negative; that is they are also "work junkies," unfortunates lamentably addicted to their work. These people find joy and fulfillment in their work roles, from which they nonetheless seem compulsively unable to take any real holiday.

The positive, nonaddictive side of workaholism bears a strong resemblance to occupational devotion. Thus the modern work ethic—most generally put that hard work is good—is manifested in at least two main ways among other ways: workaholism and occupational devotion. Generally speaking, the scope of the latter has shrunk in some ways. It has been buffeted by such forces as occupational deskilling and degradation (e.g., Braverman 1974), industrial restructuring (e.g., downsizing), deindustrialization (e.g., plant closure and relocation), failed job improvement programs (e.g., the Human Relations and Quality of Work movements, Applebaum [1992, 587]), and overwork, whether required by employers or sought by workers craving extra income. Nevertheless, certain forms of devotion are more evident today than heretofore, seen for instance, in the rise of the independent consultant and the part-time professional.

But, alas, occupational devotion is a neologism, necessitated partly by the fact that workaholism, as a term, has through careless lay usage become corrupted and distorted to mean, now even for some scientists (e.g., Killinger 1997; Sonnenberg 1996), compulsion to work. Perhaps such distortion should have been expected, given that this sense of "ism" refers to the conduct of a class of people seen as much like that of another class, namely, people suffering from alcoholism. In this metaphorical stance compulsive workers, who toil well beyond providing for a reasonable lifestyle, are believed to find little of intrinsic worth in their work, instead they find only an irresistible impulse to engage in it. Workaholism will refer in this book only to this negative meaning, putting it thus beyond the scope of a positive sociology. These days most people speak most of the time about workaholics as work addicts, either forgetting or overlooking the fact that occupational devotees also exist. Still some of those they casually label workaholic may well be devotees in both thought and action.

In the original, Machlowitzian version of the workaholism thesis, the passion people have for their work is explained, albeit in contradictory terms, by, in part, their love for it and by, in part, their addiction to it. Love suggests workers are attracted to their jobs by such rewards as self-fulfillment, self-expression, self-enrichment, and the like. These lead to deep occupational fulfillment. In contrast, addiction suggests workers are dragged to work by forces beyond their control. No rewards here of the sort just mentioned, rather there is only the compelling need to work and for many to make money, often in amounts well beyond those required for comfortable living.

And, over the years, the term workaholism has come to mean exclusively this, with reference to a passion for work having rather quickly fallen into disfavor, perhaps because it so difficult these days to locate instances of it.

In sum, workaholism, occupational devotion, and the work ethic are, with some overlap in meaning, complementary orientations. The work ethic states that work is good, and it is important to do a good job while at it. Workaholism (adulterated version) states that, for some people, working is a compulsion. Occupational devotion includes the condition that work is intrinsically rewarding. The first and third are comprised of both attitudes and values, while the second seriously overextends the first, turning attitude and value into an uncontrollable drive to make money or simply do one's job, if not both. Combined, all three orientations constitute a substantial replacement of the Protestant ethic.

History of Leisure Activity

That part of the history of leisure activity bearing most directly on the first principles of leisure is the ideal of "rational recreation," which the nineteenth-century middle-class reformers hoped to impose on the urban working class of their day. They believed that "leisure activities should be controlled, ordered, and improving" (Cunningham 1980, 90), qualities not typically found in the free-time behavior of laboring men. More particularly, recreation was viewed as rational when it fosters personal acquisitions like self-improvement and self-enrichment and, based on these, enhanced self-expression and personal and social identity. Pursuing excellence in, say, amateur tennis, hobbyist stamp collecting, or volunteer work with youth exemplifies such recreation. Whereas nonrational recreation—leisure that leads to no such acquisitions but, rather, is done for pure pleasure—is the classificatory home of casual activities like napping, strolling in the park, and of course, watching television (primarily for entertainment).

Cross (1990, chap. 7) observes that, during much of the nineteenth century, employers and upwardly mobile employees looked on "idleness" as threatening industrial development and social stability. The reformers in their midst sought to eliminate this menace by, among other approaches, attempting to build bridges to the "dangerous classes" in the new cities and, by this means, to transform them in the image of the middle class. This led to efforts to impose (largely rural) middle-class values on this group, while trying to instill a desire to engage in rational recreation—in modern terms, serious leisure—and consequently to undertake less casual leisure.

Part of this reform revolved around attempts to get the working classes to embrace an ethic of self-control, individualism, and respectability, which did not, however, meet with great success. But more central to the rational recreation movement were projects that facilitated serious leisure, such as establishing museums, opening reading rooms, and providing spaces for athletic and performing arts activities. Some of these activities were organized by working men's social clubs, established in part for this reason, and some were organized by their employers. Many of today's urban parks and museums owe their existence to this movement.

Cross (1990, 99) concluded that "it is doubtful whether workers' leisure became more respectable in precisely the ways endorsed by reformist patrons." He noted that the social classes may have walked the bridges that the patrons built, but no new understanding resulted. Yet, even if most wage earners failed to replace traditional casual pleasures with rational satisfactions, many added aspects of the reformers' program to their leisure repertory. "The result was in part a more privatized, more sedate, and more universal recreational culture. For some individuals, rational recreation may have helped to create a personality suitable to the competitive upwardly mobile society of the Victorian city" (100).

The Rise of Modern Amateurism

As professionalization spreads from one occupation to another, what was once considered play in some of these spheres is evolving quietly, inevitably, and unnoticeably into a new form—one best-named *modern amateurism.* Modern amateurism has been raising alongside those occupations where some participants in the occupation are now able to make a substantial living from it and, consequently, to devote themselves to it as a vocation rather than an avocation. Although there are possibly others, we know that science, entertainment, sport and games, as well as fine arts, are major occupational areas where work was once purely play and where modern amateurism is now a parallel development.

What has been happening is that those who play at the activities constituting the core of these occupations are being overrun in significance, if not in numbers, by professionals and amateurs. It is a process that seems to unfold as follows. As opportunities for full-time pursuit of a skill or activity gradually appear, people with even an average aptitude for such skills are able to develop them to a level observably higher than that of the typical part-time participant. With today's mass availability of professional performances (or products), whatever the field, new standards of excellence soon confront all participants, professional or not. Although the performances of professionals are frequently impressive, no category of participant is more impressed than that of the nonprofessionals who, through direct experience, know the activity intimately. Indeed, once they become aware of professional standards, all they have accomplished seems mediocre by comparison. They are thus faced with a critical choice in their careers as participants: either they restrict identification with the activity so as to remain largely unaffected by such invidious comparisons, or they identify sufficiently with it to attempt to meet those standards.

With the first choice, which is still common, the part-time participant remains a player, dabbler, or dilettante. Following Huizinga (1955), we can say that leisure of that type lacks necessity, obligation, and utility and will be produced with a disinterestedness that sets it, as an activity, apart from the participants' ordinary, real lives. The second choice, also common and becoming more so, impels part-time participants away from play toward the pursuit of durable benefits. The road to these benefits, however, passes through necessity, seriousness, commitment, and agreeable obligation as expressed by regimentation (e.g., rehearsals and practice) and systematization (e.g., schedules and organization), and progresses on to the status of modern amateur for some and professional for others. Godbout (1990) has noted this trend in what he calls the "*professionnalisation des loisirs*" (professionalization of leisure), basically its regimentation or systematization.

Players of old in sport and music, and quite possibly other fields, were referred to as "gentleman" (very few were women). But first Huizinga (1955, chap. 12), and then Stone (1971, 48) commented on the gradual disappearance of such players from sport. Indeed, it is an ongoing process. Barzun (1956, 61) discusses this transformation in music.

There was a time, furthermore, when players and amateurs (probably differences existed between them even then) were alone in their activities—without professionals to compete against, model themselves after, or simply mingle with. In fact, the early history of many contemporary professions (e.g., astronomy, music, soccer) was made up exclusively of amateurs, the only people practicing the professions in their day. In effect, these endeavors were too new, too little in demand, or too underdeveloped to be pursued as livelihoods. In other words, when their fields began, a number of astronomers, archaeologists, teachers, musicians, painters, jugglers, bowlers, soccer players, and so forth earned their living doing something else; clearly, however, they were experts, by standards of the day, in their respective areas of leisure.

In some fields amateurism was an honorable tradition, and attempts at full-time employment, to say nothing of professionalization, were met with derision. It was considered despicable to make money this way. But, as the two categories of participant began to diverge, it remains to be discovered just how many fields existed in which amateurs could be distinguished from professionals by social class. Whannel (1983, 43) notes that, in the nineteenth century, those who played sport for money belonged to the lower class, whereas those who played purely for enjoyment belonged to the upper class. For many years, informal, sometimes even formal, arrangements prevented the different classes of teams and individuals from competing with one another. Today, however, all but the poorest classes participate in amateur activities, even if a few activities disproportionately attract the rich (e.g., polo) or the working classes (e.g., dirt bike racing).

As professionals began to dominate a field pioneered by amateurs, however, a transformation in the meaning of "amateur" seems to have occurred. During this period, old definitions clung tenaciously, merging in common discourse with new ones springing up to describe modern amateurism. From a research standpoint, the result was emergence of the idea of amateur, now an everyday term, though one defined with annoying imprecision in contemporary dictionaries.

The entries in *Webster's Unabridged Dictionary* exemplify the problem. Amateurs, for instance, are defined, in one sense, as devotees who love a particular activity; in another sense as dilettantes or dabblers. Dilettantes, on the other hand, are defined, in the first sense, as lovers of the arts and, in the second, as people with discrimination or taste. Consider, also, the logical difficulties posed by yet another sense of "amateur"—that is, the inexperienced person (or player)—and the patent fact that devotees of an activity quite naturally put in much time at it, thereby achieving remarkable competence (i.e., modern amateurs).

The Rise of Hobbies

Knowledge about the history of hobbies centers mainly on industrialized capitalist Europe and North America from mid-nineteenth century. Steven Gelber (1999) observes that industrialism separated work from leisure such that employment became more work-like and nonwork became more problematic. Americans, he said, responded in two ways to the threat posed by leisure as potential mischief caused by idle hands. Reformers tried to eliminate, or at least restrict access to, inappropriate activity, while encouraging people to seek socially approved free-time outlets. Hobbies and other serious leisure pursuits were high on the list of such outlets. Like work, leisure had to be productive. Hobbies were also particularly valued, because they bridged especially well the worlds of work and home. And both sexes found them appealing, albeit mostly not the same ones. Nevertheless, before approximately 1880, before becoming defined as productive use of free time, hobbies were considered "dangerous obsessions."

Temporal Space

So far we have been looking at leisure as free time, but with a special definition of free time. Here, *free time consists of the minutes, hours, days, and so on not spent meeting disagreeable obligation, or at least the most constraining of them.* That is we will see in Chapter 4 that serious and project-based leisure sometimes have some disagreeable obligations, but they are not odious enough to force the participant to abandon the activity in question. We might refer to this aspect of leisure as "time virtually free of disagreeable obligation," but the locution is clumsy. Thus we will stay with "free time," as just redefined, with the hope that conventional definitions of it will not undermine this new meaning.

Nevertheless, most scholars guided by the temporal approach see leisure time much more narrowly: as that time not spent making a living. This conceptualization, however, fails to cover the time devoted to nonwork obligations (discussed in the next chapter) as well as that given to devotee work. Time-use studies, which examine the proportions of time spent at leisure vis-à-vis work, exemplify well this narrower temporal definition of leisure (e.g., Cushman, Veal, and Zuzanek 2005; Robinson and Godbey 1997). Variations in the proportion of time spent at work (all types) and away from it in different countries and different parts of the population within countries are among the most intensely scrutinized subjects in leisure studies.

Temporal space may be further understood in terms of "discretionary time commitment" (Stebbins 2006a). This kind of commitment refers to the noncoerced, allocation of a certain number of minutes, hours, days, or other measure of time that a person devotes, or would like to devote, to carrying out an activity. Such commitment is both process and product. That is people either set (process) their own time commitments (products) or willingly accept such commitments (i.e., agreeable obligations) set for them by others. It follows that disagreeable obligations, which are invariably forced on people by others or by circumstances, fail to constitute discretionary time commitments. In short, discretionary time commitment finds expression in leisure and in the agreeable sides of work.

Note, however, that we can, and sometimes do, allocate time to carrying out disagreeable activities, whether at work or outside it. Such commitments—call them *coerced time commitments*—are, obviously, not discretionary. Hence they fall beyond the scope of this discussion and, with some interesting exceptions, beyond the scope of leisure (i.e., some leisure costs—see the most recent discussion of them in Stebbins [2007a, chap. 1]—can be understood as coerced time commitments).

More generally we commonly speak of past, present, and future time commitments (discretionary and coerced) at work, leisure, and in the realm of nonwork obligations. The kinds of time commitments people make help shape their work and leisure lifestyles, and constitute part of the patterning of those lifestyles. In leisure the nature of such commitments varies substantially across its three forms: serious, casual, and project-based leisure.

Varying Time Commitments

Generally speaking, serious leisure requires its participants to allocate more time than participants in the other two forms, if for no other reason, than that, of the three, it seems most likely to be pursued over the longest span of time. In addition, certain qualities of serious leisure, including especially perseverance, commitment, effort, and career, tend to make amateurs, hobbyists, and volunteers especially cognizant of how they allocate their free time, the amount of that time they use for their serious leisure, and the ways they accomplish this.

There are many examples. Amateur and hobbyist activities based on the development and polishing of physical skills (e.g., learning how to juggle, figure skate, make quilts, play the piano) require the aspiring entertainer, skater, quilter, and so on to commit a fair amount of time on a regular basis, sometimes over several years, to acquiring and polishing necessary skills. And once acquired, the skills and related physical conditioning must be maintained through continuous use. Additionally some serious leisure enthusiasts take on (agreeable) obligations (Stebbins 2000a) that demand their presence at certain places at certain times (e.g., rehearsals, matches, meetings, events). But most important, the core activity, which is the essence of a person's serious leisure, is so attractive that this individual very much wants to set aside sufficient time to engage in it.

In other words, serious leisure often borders on being *uncontrollable.* It engenders in its practitioners a desire to pursue the activity beyond the time or the money (if not both) available for it. So, even though hobbies such as collecting stamps or making furniture usually have few schedules or appointments to meet, they are nonetheless enormously appealing, and as such encourage these collectors and makers to allocate, whenever possible, time for this leisure.

Project-based leisure may be accompanied by similar demands. It is a short-term, reasonably complicated, one-shot or occasional, though infrequent, creative undertaking carried out in free time, or time free of disagreeable obligation (a full discussion of this concept is presented in Chapter 4). There participants may find scheduled meetings or responsibilities, if not both, and though of short range, the condition of uncontrollability can also be a concern. But project-based leisure does not, by definition, involve developing, polishing, and maintaining physical skills, this being one of the key differences in use of discretionary time separating it from serious leisure. Furthermore, with project-based leisure comes a unique sense of time allocation: time use is more or less intense but limited to a known and definite period on the calendar (e.g., when the athletic games are over, when the stone wall is built, when the surprise birthday party has taken place). Indeed, one of the attractions of projects for some people is that no long-term commitment of time is foreseen.

Finally, casual leisure may, in its own way, generate time commitments, as in the desire to set aside an hour each week to watch a television program or participate as often as possible in a morning neighborhood coffee klatch. Further some casual leisure, famously watching television, is attractive, in part, because it is often available on a moment's notice—call it "spontaneous discretionary time commitment"; it can fill in gaps between discretionary and coerced time commitments, and in the process, stave off boredom. Additionally casual volunteering commonly has temporal requirements, as in joining for the weekend an environmental clean-up crew, serving on Thanksgiving Day free meals to the poor, and collecting money for a charity by going door-to-door or soliciting on a street corner.

Moreover, in fashioning their leisure lifestyles, people blend and coordinate their participation and allocation of free time in one or more of the three forms. In this regard, some people try to organize their free time in such a way that they approach, as they define it, an "optimal leisure lifestyle" (Stebbins 2000b). The term refers to the deeply rewarding and interesting pursuit during free time of one or more substantial, absorbing forms of serious leisure, complemented by judicious amounts of casual leisure or project-based leisure or both. People find optimal leisure lifestyles (OLLs) by partaking of leisure activities that individually and in combination help them to realize their human potential, leading thereby to self-fulfillment and enhanced well-being and quality of life.

Boring Time

One main problem inherent in this conceptualization of space, whether narrowed to include only work or broadened to include non-work obligations, is that people may be bored during their free time. Boredom can result from inactivity ("nothing to do") or from activity, which alas, has become uninteresting, unstimulating (a common lament about some entertainment television). The same can, of course, happen at work and in obligated nonwork settings. Since boredom is a decidedly negative state of mind, it may be argued following the definition just presented that, logically, it is not leisure at all (Stebbins 2003). For leisure is typically conceived of as a positive state of mind, composed of, among other sentiments, pleasant expectations and recollections of activities and situations (Kaplan 1960, 22–25). But it may happen that leisure expectations turn out to be unrealistic, and we get bored (or perhaps angry, frightened, or embarrassed) with the activity in question, transforming it in our view into something quite other than leisure. And all this may occur in free time, which exemplifies well how such time covers a broader area of life than leisure does, which is nested within.

Comments so far have centered primarily on individuals and their dislike for boredom as coerced, unpleasant obligation. Still, this emotional state, it should be noted, can also have far-reaching personal and social consequences, some of them positive, some of them negative. Cohen-Gewerc (2001) argues that boredom can become a gateway for creative leisure. Individually, it can stimulate people to discover their inner selves, and thereby emancipate themselves from boring tasks and roles. Collectively, widespread boredom in a given group or population can spawn significant social change. William Ralph Inge, twentieth-century British churchman, wrote that "the effect of boredom on a large scale in history is underestimated. It is a main cause of revolutions, and would soon bring to an end all the static Utopias and the farmyard civilization of the Fabians." It is not just that people dislike being bored, but also that they sometimes get angry with their situation and are therefore driven to shape the world such that they can escape it (and perhaps punish those felt to have caused it). Most generally put, boredom can be an incentive to action to alleviate it.

Geographic Space

Leisure space conceived of in geographic terms refers to the places where leisure activities are pursued. These places may be natural or artificial or a combination of both. Natural spaces include largely unmodified aspects of public and private land, waterways, waterfronts, lakes and oceans, and the air above the earth. True, any of these spaces may be polluted and, as such, modified. But modification of this sort does not make them artificial.

The artificial spaces are *built* by humans. They include indoor and outdoor swimming pools, basketball courts, and ice rinks. All manner of productions and displays in the fine and entertainment arts occur in circumstances completely or substantially artificial (including symphonic concerts by the lake or the sea or in the mountains). Then there is the built environment that is the shopping mall, strip, or street that is patronized as casual leisure in the form of browsing and the possibility of buying something for the fun of it.

David Crouch (2006) adds to this statement on the scope of geographic space two other "components" (my term). One is virtual space, or cyberspace, which is artificial, too, having an unfathomable vastness shared only with the natural space beyond Earth. The other component—the body—is natural, and of all the geographic spaces, is possibly the one most given to evaluation and signification by the individual and others.

Crouch summarizes the importance of understanding leisure in terms of geographic space:

> Leisure happens, is produced in spaces. These spaces may be material, and related to concrete locations. Yet the spaces, and therefore geographies, of leisure may be metaphorical, even imaginative. Imaginative spaces are not merely in the virtual space of contemporary nature but also in the imagination of consumer and the representations of the agencies providing in producing leisure sites: visual culture and other narratives of communication.... Space, then, can be important in metaphorically "shaping," contextualizing leisure and commercial and public policy prefiguring of the meaning of leisure sites, and the leisure experience may be transformed by the way in which individuals encounter those spaces and activities. (Crouch 2006, 127)

In the language of this book leisure activities occur in geographic space in the broad terms just described, which helps shape those activities and give them meaning for the individual participant.

Geography, at least in its human/cultural branch, does formally recognize the importance of leisure as part of its conceptual framework. Johnston et al. (2000, 444–45) in their dictionary of human geography fill two pages on the subject, presenting a decently wide-ranging coverage of some of the definitions extant in the field of leisure studies. Leisure is an important idea in urban and regional planning, where recreational facilities are among the many buildings and areas that must be designed. In physical geography outdoor leisure activities, which obviously take place in some kind of space, are a key element in the training of outdoor guides. And leisure, geography, and tourism make fine theoretic bedfellows. Crouch's (2000) study of the link between leisure and geography in Britain shows well the degree of conceptual integration of these two fields.

Additionally Li (n.d.) writes about the importance of leisure in the "geographic account" of everyday life.

> This account clarifies the content and the key theme of the geographical inquiry on everyday life through an examination of how geographical concepts are actually perceived and appraised by people in their everyday lives. It suggests that geography of everyday life entails two fundamental categories of human life—place and time, as well as human selves as beings which conceptualize and act in the place and the time, where and when everyday life occurs. This account indicates there are many fundamentally geographical aspects

to leisure study. First and foremost, our leisure life occurs in places. Leisure pursuit as part of everyday life is the plausible social context and believable personal world within which we reside. (10)

Li goes on to note that we derive a sense of self and identity from the geographic side of our leisure. Moreover our leisure experiences have a geographic aspect.

Nature Challenge Activities

The *nature challenge activity* (NCA), a distinctive type of outdoor pursuit that, in one form or another, appeals to all ages (Davidson and Stebbins 2011). The NCA is leisure whose core activity or activities center on meeting a natural test posed by one or more of six elements: (1) air; (2) water; (3) land; (4) animals (including birds and fish); (5) plants; and (6) ice or snow (sometimes both). A main reason for engaging in a particular NCA is to experience participation in its core activities pursued in a natural setting. In other words, while executing these activities, the special (aesthetic) appeal of the natural environment in which this process occurs simultaneously sets the challenge the participant seeks. At the same time many participants tend to consume the goods and services related to their NCAs in ways that are environmental friendly. Of course, as we will point out in many places in this book, other important reasons also exist for such participation, as suggested by the geographic, economic, and social dimensions of the use of nature. Moreover, some NCAs even have a counterpart in a line of devotee work (e.g., professional sport fishermen, mountain guides, nature photographers).

Outings in nature considered as leisure activity constitute a main geographic way in which people in the West of today use their free time. In the study of NCAs, nature is regarded as any natural setting *perceived* by users as at most only minimally modified by human beings. In its most general manifestation, nature thus defined is composed of one of more of the aforementioned six elements. The perceptual qualification just made is important, since nature lovers may feel they are in nature that, for example, is nonetheless imperceptibly polluted. In fact, all six elements risk being sullied by this unwelcome process. Or nature lovers might recognize that pollution exists, but discount it as insignificant or unavoidable. For instance, certain kinds of trees might be dying, precipitated by an infestation of an insect, but a hike or cross-country ski through this region is still enjoyable, in part because the hikers or skiers are enthralled with other aspects of nature viewed by them as pristine (e.g., the snow, forest, geography, and clean air).

Westerners have unequal access to nature, with, it would appear, those living in cities being, as a group, the most deprived in this respect. Much of city life takes place in substantially, if not entirely, artificial surroundings. Subways, buildings (notwithstanding the occasional plant or water fountain inside), streets and sidewalks (even those lined with trees), bridges and the like are the antithesis of nature as just defined it. Furthermore, city parks, walk ways along rivers, public gardens and similar developments are only marginally less artificial. And the built environment is as prominent in small towns and even on farms to the extent that the latter abut one another to form a contiguous stretch of land modified by humans. This is evident in roads, buildings, planted crops, and fenced pasture. In all these settings nature has been, for the most part, far more than minimally modified for human use.

Conclusions

Let us return to the matter of the uniqueness of leisure, discussed in some detail at the end of the preceding chapter. First, note that the social institution of leisure is unique, compared with the other institutions comprising modern society. A sizeable book could be written on the configurations of values, norms, roles, activities, patterns of behavior, and emergent set of problems to be solved as related to leisure in a given society. That is such a book could be written if only leisure studies know enough about these phenomena as related to a representative sample of leisure activities there. All we can say with certainty, today, about the uniqueness of the institution of leisure is that such configurations do exist and that a vast program of research is needed to discover their actual expressions and distributions. Nonetheless the leisure institution constitutes a fourth unique principle of leisure.

How about the other two spaces of leisure? Are they unique? I argued in Chapter 1 and in the section in this chapter on temporal space that free time spent away from unpleasant obligation meets this criterion. This leaves the question of whether geographic leisure space may be considered a unique property of leisure.

The answer to this question is yes, which however, requires some elucidation. Let us proceed, *à la* Li above, from the subjective view of geographic space, space as users understand it. Thus there is a multitude of places and spaces popularly thought of as being used exclusively for one or more leisure activities. They are *pure* geographic leisure spaces. Within this type at this point, we lack a neat classification of such places and spaces, so a miscellaneous list of examples must suffice. They include: playgrounds, scenic vistas, camping sites, tennis courts, cross-country ski trails, cinemas, beaches, pool halls, dance floors, gift shops, and areas where books, CDs, DVDs, and the like are sold. In all such places a few people also make a living operating or maintaining them, which unless it is devotee work, is not leisure. But they are relatively invisible, thereby helping to perpetuate the impression that they exist purely for leisure, that they are essentially leisure spaces.

By contrast, there are places devoted to providing some kind of leisure where the remunerated workers involved loom large, identified here as *professional-service* geographic leisure space. In this category we find strip joints, gambling establishments, concert venues (jazz, rock, classical music, etc.), massage parlors, race tracks, fashion shows, sports stadia, tour buses (with tour guide at the microphone), among others. These are places of both work (sometimes including devotee work) and leisure, an arrangement obvious to all who frequent them. Clients or publics come to them for satisfaction or, more rarely, self-fulfillment as provided directly by trained, remunerated workers. Moreover, the clients and publics expect the workers to provide an acceptable service (i.e., it should meet standards). In brief, this type of space is essentially one of mixed work and leisure, a definition shared by all who participate in it.

It might be argued here that since, some of the workers are occupational devotees, professional-service geographic leisure space is really just a special version of the pure type. True, this book places occupational devotion under the leisure heading of serious pursuits, and devotees look on their work spaces as places for realizing these pursuits. But the clients and publics generally fail to see this motivational subtly. Rather, when in a professional-service geographic leisure space, they pay workers to give them a satisfying or fulfilling product. That the latter love their work as if they were serious leisure participants is not commonly recognized by the former.

Still, other geographic spaces are used as locations for either pleasure or work. Call them *mixed* geographic leisure spaces. Main examples include bars, restaurants, libraries, and museums. Thus, some people go to a bar or restaurant to have a sociable conversation and enjoy drink or food, others go to discuss a business deal, and still others to make a living in these places as servers, bartenders, or cooks. Likewise some patrons go to museums and libraries for casual or serious leisure reading or viewing of displays, whereas as others go there to get information related to their job (e.g., school teachers, historians, researchers). Many of the workers employed by these establishments do provide a service, but in contrast with the professional-service providers, neither they nor the service are the center of attention. In short, professional-service and mixed spaces serve other important interests besides leisure, and therefore they cannot be counted as uniquely geographic leisure spaces.

We may say that geographic leisure space constitutes a fifth unique principle of leisure, but only when that space is of the pure type. It must be further recognized that a great deal of leisure activity occurs outside this context, in spaces that are the scene of both work and leisure, spaces not essentially or exclusively used for passing free time. As for cyberspace it may become evident, upon careful research, that it offers pure spaces, as possibly manifested according to website or type of website. It seems unlikely, however, that we will be able to say the same about bodily space, which seems to lend itself to use in all three domains of human activity and not just that of leisure. These domains are the subject of the next chapter.

3

Three Domains of Activity

On the *activity* level, the great proportion of everyday life can be conceptualized as being experienced in one of three domains: work, leisure, and nonwork obligation. At first blush it might seem that all of life can be conceptualized thus. Still, while discussing activity in Chapter 1, we saw that experiences we must undergo entirely against our will fail to fit the definition of activity presented there. Both fail to qualify as activities. As pointed out the ends sought in these unwanted experiences are those of other people, as they pursue their activities. The "victims" of those activities lack agency, unless as noted, they can manage to counterattack with an activity intended as resistance. One might ask at this point if our existence is not more complicated than this. Indeed it is, for each of the three is itself enormously complex, and there is also some significant overlap in the domains.

The domain approach is a prism through which to view the institutional space of leisure. In its own special way it elaborates the institutional definition of leisure. This said the idea of domain is distinctive enough to be treated of separately, since it is rare in the social sciences to view everyday life as unfolding in these three different but interrelated spheres. That is, the pursuit of activities in these three domains is framed in a wide range of social conditions, some of which, at that level of analysis, blur domainal boundaries. For example, if the state mandates that no one may work more than thirty-five hours a week, this will affect the typical amount of time spent in activities in the work domain vis-à-vis those in the domains of leisure and nonwork obligation. Or consider the condition of poverty. For the impoverished its components of hunger, disease, malnutrition, and unemployment largely efface the nonwork and leisure domains, forcing these people into the full-time activity of survival (subsistence-level work). Third, on the cultural plane, some groups (e.g., religious, communal) stress the importance of altruism and its expression in volunteering. Volunteering here is leisure activity, which, however, loses this quality when experienced as coercion. The feeling of *having* to "volunteer" transforms such activity into a kind of nonwork obligation. Examples of this nature are found throughout this book; they constitute a mechanism for facilitating understanding of the positive activities of life from the angle of the relevant social and personal conditions framing them.

Bear in mind that activities, when considered from the domainal perspective, are of the general variety, such as tennis or collecting stamps (leisure domain), teaching school or driving a taxi (work domain), and going through airport security or putting on makeup (nonwork obligation). As pursuits they are part of the institutions of work and leisure (nonwork obligation is not an institution). Put otherwise they form part of the context (e.g., cultural expectations, institutionalized relations and relationships, organizational arrangements) in which life is carried out. On the other hand, the central thoughts and actions that people have and do to enact these general activities were labeled earlier as core activities. They are a part of the leisure experience—in fact an essential part of it—part of the individual approach to defining leisure.

Leisure

The leisure domain is only summarily introduced in this chapter, since it will be covered far more thoroughly in the next chapter in which the SLP is set out. In the main it is important to remember the first principles of leisure, so as to see in greatest clarity how this domain differs from the other two. Three of the principles were pulled from the dictionary-style definition presented in Chapter 1: uncoerced, contextually framed activity engaged in during free time, which people want to do and, using their abilities and resources, actually do in either a satisfying or a fulfilling way (or both). This definition, however, encompasses both general activity and the essential core activities within. Leisure as a domain, as a distinctive part of the institution of leisure (the fourth principle), focuses attention primarily on the first of these two types. Geographic leisure space of the pure variety constitutes the fifth principle.

The statement in the next chapter on the SLP contains scant mention of today's new leisure. Yet, new leisure is all around us, and as such, cuts a prominent figure in modern life. When we think of leisure we also think of the new, not infrequently bizarre, free-time activities people engage in these days. It is thus a distinctive feature of the leisure space.

New Leisure

New leisure is any activity of recent invention undertaken in free time, in the sense that a number of people in a region, nation, or larger sociocultural unit have only lately taken it up as a pastime (more fully treated of in Stebbins [2009c]). In fact, the activity might have been, until some point in history, entirely local, say, enjoyed for many years but only in an isolated small town, ethnic enclave or minority group (e.g., lacrosse, archery). Then the activity gains a following in the surrounding region, nation, or beyond. Most often, however, new leisure activities appear to have been recently invented, albeit commonly with one or more older, established activities as models. New leisure activities are a diverse lot, found in serious, casual, and project-based forms. They also appear to be invented at a much greater rate today than earlier, in significant part because of processes leading to globalization.

This definition of new leisure is admittedly vague. Such terminology as "recent," "a number of," and "established leisure" lack precision, which will only be possible to achieve with careful exploratory research on these activities. The definition above is thus tentative, but hopefully clear enough to focus the following discussion. On the other hand, the idea of invention is clearer, even if joined here with the condition of recency to emphasize the contemporary sociocultural context within which new activities are conceived.

There are several notable properties of new leisure, one being its role in globalization. These days word of an interesting new activity spreads quickly through the mass media and over the Internet. Aided by the growing universality of a reading knowledge of English, human interest articles in this language on new leisure appear from time to time in various newspapers and magazines. Enthusiasts also use the Internet, forming websites, writing blogs, and establishing electronic discussion groups. This broad, complex interconnectedness makes possible, depending on the activity, extralocal competitions, conferences, expositions, and most probably more informal get-togethers such as meetings of like-minded folk in restaurants and private homes and by e-mail.

Furthermore, leisure inventions are important as vehicles of human creativity. The invention of the snowboard and snowboarding illustrates how this works (see Stebbins 2009c, 79–80). There are myriad ways in which people across the world invent objects, practices, and activities, with new leisure being but one vehicle for this. Nonetheless that leisure invention occurs frequently shows the significance of leisure in the lives of a good number of people the world over. Indeed, of all institutions in a modern society, the leisure institution could be shown to be the arena for the largest number of the society's inventions. It follows that new leisure may also be symptomatic of social change.

Many of the new leisure activities can serve as a resource in leisure education. Part of the mandate of practitioners in this field is to familiarize clients and students with a range of personally accessible leisure activities and then encourage them to pursue those for which they have both taste and aptitude. New serious leisure activities may also be appealing because they offer an uncommon identity as accomplished participant in one of them. Additionally new leisure in general could turn out, upon closer examination, to be an especially effective mechanism by which to encourage people to set aside more free time or to use their existing free time in more personally rewarding or fulfilling ways. In sum, new leisure can also figure prominently in achieving an agreeable work/life balance.

Work

Work, says Applebaum (1992, x), has no satisfactory definition, since the idea relates to all human activities. That caveat aside, he sees work, among other ways, as performance of useful activity (making things, performing services) done as all or part of sustaining life, as a livelihood. Some people are remunerated for their work, whereas others get paid in kind or directly keep body and soul together with the fruits of their labor (e.g., subsistence farming, hunting, fishing). Work, thus defined, is as old as humankind, since all save a few privileged people have always had to seek a livelihood. The same may be said for leisure, to the extent that some free time has always existed after work. Today, in the West, most work of the kind considered here is remunerated, but the nonremunerated variety is evident, too. The most celebrated example of the latter is house work, but there are also livelihood-related activities that we tend to define as nonwork obligation (e.g., do-it-yourself house repairs, money-saving dress making). Work, as just defined, is activity people have to do, if they are to meet their economic needs. And, though some exceptions are examined later in this section, most people do not particularly like their work. If, for example, their livelihood were somehow guaranteed, they would take up more pleasant activities, assuming of course, they are aware of them.

For many Westerners working time is a major part of everyday life, commonly eating up many hours a week from age seventeen or eighteen to sixty-five or seventy, and nowadays, even older. So work is not only this person's livelihood, it is also a major component of his or her lifestyle. But to keep work in perspective, we need to underscore further how much of life for the Westerner is actually not work at all, in that it consists of activity other than that devoted to making a living. In this regard, Applebaum's definition overlooks the fact that making things and performing services can also occur as serious leisure, as any furniture maker or volunteer, for example, would happily acknowledge.

Moreover, work is not even a universal feature of most Westerners' life-long existence. First, during childhood and adolescence, most people are not engaged, or are engaged rather little, in work activities. Second, during their working years, some people wind up being unemployed (get fired, laid off, disabled), placing them at least temporarily outside the work force. Third, most people retire, though this status is fuzzy because some of them remain partially employed during some or all of this stage of life.

Fourth, even when working full-time in the West as measured by a nation's average work week, workers typically have considerably more free time than work time. That is we all exist in a week of 168 hours. Let us estimate that, on average, seventy of those hours go for sleep and bodily maintenance (including fitness activity) taken after a modern thirty-six-hour average workweek. According to this formula, sixty-two hours remain for family, leisure, and nonwork obligations. The *Economist* (2006) reports that the time working-age Americans, for example, devote to leisure activities has risen by four to eight hours a week over the past four decades. This pattern is broken by those who decide (or are forced) to work longer hours or are pressed to put in excessive time meeting nonwork obligations.

What is critical in all this for the idea of leisure is the presence of a small proportion of the working population in the West who find it difficult to separate their work and leisure. These workers, for whom the line between the two domains is blurred, do rely on their work as a livelihood, but nevertheless are also "occupational devotees" (Stebbins 2004a). That is they feel a powerful *occupational devotion*, or strong, positive attachment to a form of self-enhancing work, where the sense of achievement is high and the core activity is endowed with such intense appeal that the line between this work and leisure is virtually erased. In recognition of this essentially leisure aspect of devotee work, it was lumped in Chapter 1 with serious leisure under the heading of Serious Pursuits. Because devotee work is essentially leisure, it will not be discussed further here, but instead elaborated on in the next chapter.

Nonwork Obligation

Obligation outside that experienced while pursuing a livelihood is terribly understudied (much of it falls under the heading of family and/or domestic life, while obligatory communal involvements are also possible) and sometimes seriously misunderstood (as in coerced "volunteering"). To speak of obligation, is to speak not about how people are prevented from entering certain leisure activities—the object of much of research on leisure constraints—but about how people fail to define a given activity as leisure or redefine it as other than leisure, as an unpleasant obligation. Obligation is both a state of mind, an attitude—a person feels obligated—and a form of behavior—he must carry out a particular course of action, engage in a particular activity. But even while obligation is substantially mental and behavioral, it roots, too, in the social and cultural world of the obligated actor. Consequently, we may even speak of a culture of obligation that takes shape around many work, leisure, and nonwork activities (to be discussed further in Chapter 3).

Obligation fits with leisure in at least two ways: leisure may include certain agreeable obligations and the third domain of life—nonwork obligation—consists of disagreeable requirements capable of shrinking the leisure space. *Agreeable obligation* is very much a part of some leisure, evident when such obligation accompanies positive commitment to an activity that evokes pleasant memories and expectations (these two are essential features of leisure, Kaplan [1960, 22–25]). Still, it might be argued that agreeable obligation in leisure is not really felt as obligation, since the participant wants to do the activity anyway. But my research in serious leisure suggests a more complicated picture. My respondents knew that they were supposed to be at a certain place or do a certain thing and knew that they had to make this a priority in their day-to-day living (this exemplifies discretionary time commitment, Chapter 3). They not only wanted to do this, they were also required to do it; other activities and demands could wait. At times, the respondent/s intimates objected to the way he or she prioritized everyday commitments, and this led to friction, creating costs for the first that somewhat diluted the rewards of the leisure in question. Agreeable obligation is also found in devotee work and the other two forms of leisure, though possibly least so in casual leisure.

On the other hand, *disagreeable obligation* has no place in leisure, because, among other reasons, it fails to leave the participant with a pleasant memory or expectation of the activity. Rather it is the stuff of the third domain: nonwork obligation. This domain is the classificatory home of all we must do that we would rather avoid that is not related to work (including moonlighting). So far I have been able to identify three types.

> *Unpaid labor*: activities people do themselves even though services exist which they could hire to carry them out. These activities include mowing the lawn, house work, shoveling the sidewalk, preparing the annual income tax return, do-it-yourself, and a myriad of obligations to friends and family (e.g., caring for a sick relative, helping a friend move to another home, arranging a funeral).
>
> *Unpleasant tasks*: required activities for which no commercial services exist or, if they exist, most people would avoid using them. Such activities are exemplified in checking in and clearing security at airports, attending a meeting on a community problem, walking the dog each day, driving in city traffic (in this discussion, beyond that related to work), and errands, including routine grocery shopping. There are also obligations to family and friends in this type, among them, driving a child to soccer practice and mediating familial quarrels. Many of the "chores" of childhood fall in this category. Finally, activities sometimes mislabeled as volunteering are, in fact, disagreeable obligations from which the individual senses no escape. For example, some parents feel this way about coaching their children's sports teams or about helping out with a road trip for the youth orchestra in which their children play.
>
> *Self-care*: disagreeable activities designed to maintain or improve in some way the physical or psychological state of the individual. They include getting a haircut, putting on cosmetics, doing health-promoting exercises, going to the dentist, and undergoing a physical examination. Personal and family counseling also fall within this type, as do the activities that accompany getting a divorce.

Some activities in these types are routine obligations, whereas others are only occasional. And, for those who find some significant measure of enjoyment in, say, grocery shopping, walking the dog, do-it-yourself, or taking physical exercise, these obligations are defined as agreeable; they are effectively leisure. Thus, what is disagreeable in the domain of nonwork obligation rests on personal interpretation of the actual or anticipated experience of an activity. So most people dislike or expect to dislike their annual physical examination, though perhaps not the hypochondriac.

Nonwork obligation, even if it tends to occupy less time than the other two domains, is not therefore inconsequential. I believe the foregoing three types give substance to this assertion. Moreover, some of them may be gendered (e.g., housework), and accordingly, occasional sources of friction and attenuated positiveness in life for all concerned. Another leading concern issuing from nonwork obligation is that it reduces further the amount of free time for leisure, in general, and for some people, time for devotee work, in particular. Such obligation can threaten the latter, because it can reduce the time occupational devotees who, enamored as they are of their core work activities, would like to put in at work as, in effect, overtime.

Interrelationship of the Domains

The three domains are distinctive entities, but they are not isolated from each other. Thus, work and leisure are intimately related in a number of ways, referred to in the next section as bridges. Nonwork obligation stands more distinctly apart from the other two, but figures heavily in discussions of balance of life's activities.

Bridging Work and Leisure

In the West, at least, it has been, and still is, common to compartmentalize work and leisure, creating spheres of life that, though interconnected in diverse ways, discourage behaving in one as though the behaving person were in the other. And not only are work and leisure customarily viewed as wholly separate, as often as not, they are also viewed as mutually antagonistic spheres of life. The rule is that people are not supposed to work when at leisure and not supposed to play when at work. The two are seen as incompatible.

There is, indeed, an undeniable logic in this institutional arrangement. Work does produce a livelihood, as in payment by money, in kind, or through various means of subsistence. Except for dependents and those who are incapacitated, unemployed, or independently wealthy, nearly everyone works, most of them doing so out of necessity. By contrast, leisure is motivated not by economic necessity but rather by a desire to pursue activity that is agreeable, activity that is fun, satisfying, fulfilling, and the like. Leisure, unlike the work most people do, is not coerced. In short, when engaged in work, its very nature tends to occlude leisure, while during free time the very nature of leisure has the same effect when we try to work there.

Logic notwithstanding, this seemingly impermeable boundary between work and leisure is, in the everyday lives of many people whether at work or in leisure, bridged in at least five significant ways. These bridges create in those who make them, during the time when the bridging occurs, a sense that the boundary separating the two spheres is blurred. There is at this moment a sense that the two are not as neatly compartmentalized as common sense would have them believe.

Work in Leisure

One bridge allowing for leisure while at work is evident in the old expression "busman's holiday," which refers to the penchant of some people who are so highly enamored of their work to pursue one or more of its core activities in their free time. The bus driver, when not on the job, was said to be so enthusiastic about the activity of driving that he—in those days it was exclusively a male occupation—took to the road during his off hours in his own car or truck for the sheer pleasure this brought. Perhaps this still happens with some bus drivers. In any case there are plenty of modern examples, among them, the accountant who volunteers to look after the accounts of a nonprofit group and the physician who serves gratis several hours each week at a clinic for the poor. Many mountain guides who, when not working, climb for pleasure, and some auto mechanics who, when off the job, spend part of their leisure time tinkering with one or more old cars. All this suggests that certain core activities of work are so attractive for these people that they even seek them beyond paid employment.

This is *spillover leisure*, as Kando and Summers (1971) referred to it many years ago. It is an extension of the job into free time and, let us be clear, not an expansion of it as part of working time. Thus, the accountant, who likes his or her core working activity, might just do more of it on the job, instead of volunteering as described above. For the same reason the guides could guide more often and the mechanics could seek remunerated overtime, thereby bringing in more money while doing what they like. But these are expansions of work, not extensions of it into the realm of leisure. As for the extensions all are, in free time, serious leisure, and the fulfillment they bring is a substantial reason for undertaking them.

A second bridge over which work comes to occupy some people's free time is that of reflection. This has been dubbed *contemplation as serious leisure*: complex reflective activity engaged in for its own sake (Stebbins 2006b). In the present discussion, however, we are looking at issues arising at work that are so complicated, challenging, and interesting that the worker is inclined to think about them, even during free time. Consistent with our definition of leisure, free-time reflection is both uncoerced and agreeable mental activity. By way of example, consider the scientist who, while at the symphony, cannot put out of her mind certain implications of recent results of a study or the social worker who, intrigued by a client's intractable familial problems, continues to think about them while he is watching television after work. This sort of contemplation as serious leisure, much like similar contemplation stimulated by leisure interests, obtrudes on other, less absorbing, leisure. Of course, the issues in question are also pondered at work, but they are too fascinating for the worker to be left there.

Leisure in Work

The bridge I shall call *interstitial leisure* refers to uncoerced activity that occurs sporadically at work in short spaces of time taken from what is formally recognized as work time, but informally treated by employees as leisure. In these interstices participants are not, for the moment, working. Nor are these spaces official breaks, such as the lunch hour or the coffee break. Such leisure seems to last only a few minutes, though it may recur, perhaps often, in the same work day (or night). The origin of these "free-time" spaces is highly varied, as the following examples suggest. Thus, interstitial leisure may take place when, during work time, someone tells others nearby a joke, initiates discussion on a nonwork-related current event, or asks about the health of a colleague's ailing spouse (on care as leisure, see Stebbins [2008b]). Workers not closely supervised may engage in interstitial leisure when, during working time and for pleasure, they daydream, read a book, work a crossword puzzle, or memorize lines of a part they have in an amateur play. The cell phone and the Internet are now notorious means for facilitating leisure in work. Much of interstitial leisure appears to be casual, though memorizing lines for a play is part of a serious leisure activity.

Interstitial leisure does not encompass joking, storytelling, inquiring about family, and so on undertaken while actually performing occupational functions. Such behavior, which is not coerced, does lighten or make more interesting certain tasks of the moment. But this leisure-like behavior is significantly constrained by those tasks and the context of their execution; the behavior does not occur in free time. Thus, the letter carrier who jokes momentarily with a householder, though he or she might find the experience pleasant, must, nonetheless, hurry off, pressed by corporate rules for maintaining rapid and efficient mail delivery. The barroom piano player might while playing talk about sport with a nightclub patron, but this divided attention weakens both activities. In other words, adding levity or relief to work tasks falls short of being true leisure, nor is it typically intended as such. More will be said about this matter below in the discussion of occupational devotion.

Lengthier leisure at work may appear in the form of agreeable projects some workers sometimes take on. Whether these are defined as leisure depends on the individual carrying them out as well as the surrounding circumstances in which this is done. For example, accepting the responsibility for organizing the office Christmas party, assuming the organizer has a real choice in the matter, is likely to be a true leisure undertaking for that person. This bridge is *project-based leisure*, which for the present discussion, however, is being experienced at work rather than in free-time, where the phenomenon was first observed and conceptualized (this form of leisure is covered in more detail in Chapter 4). Project-based leisure at work may be experienced when the organizer of the project finds enjoyment, perhaps even fulfillment, in arranging a major work-related meeting or conference, organizing the office picnic, or conducting the annual drive for donations to charity. Key in all leisure, the project-based variety included, is feeling no coercion to engage in the project. Thus, to the extent coercion to execute them is felt—the project is unappealing to the person in charge of it—it becomes still another, albeit temporary, part of the job.

We have already discussed the third kind of leisure in work—the fifth bridge—under the heading of *devotee work*. But let us explore precisely how the occupational devotee gets from serious leisure to the devotee work that it begets.

Leisure Prefigures Work

Although exceptions exist (see Stebbins 2004a, chap. 5), a large majority of today's devotee occupations actually owe their existence in one way or another to one or more serious leisure precursors. The histories of amateurism, hobbyism, and volunteerism presented in

Chapter 2 made this point in a most general way. Let us now look more closely at the details.

Amateurs Become Professionals

It was observed earlier that every professional field in art, science, sport, and entertainment made its debut with a gang of enthusiastic amateurs who pioneered the way. Thus, in all these areas the love for the core activity got its start in free time. But for some of these amateurs, their free time was too limited. It would be nice, they reasoned, were they able to engage full time in such absorbing, fulfilling, and rewarding undertakings. So once society's need for the activity caught up with the desire of some of its practitioners to pursue it at length, the emergence of the professional wing was all but ensured.

But if amateurs always have professional counterparts, the reverse, at first glance, might appear to be impossible. In other words, do professionals always have amateur counterparts? To begin, let us note that client-centered professionals are authenticated by formal licensing procedures based on specialized training, which among other things, are meant to generate for their clients the impression that they are receiving competent and certified advice and treatment. Furthermore, each profession exercises monopolistic control over who receives this training, as offered in a set of occupations that form around problematic areas of life where uncertainty is too acute to permit unfettered, free enterprise to supply the remedy. We need control in these areas, which we have granted in substantial degree to the client-centered professions. Not so, however, with the public-centered professions. They form instead in various expressive areas of life, where there is no acute uncertainty and where, as a result, no one has acquired the right of control, including even the professions themselves.

Still, client-centered professionals must be trained, and here is where amateurs (and, as noted below, sometimes volunteers) enter the picture. In particular, it is plausible to describe these trainees as "pre-professional amateurs" (Stebbins 1979, 36), who as they take courses, engage in practical work, and learn just how fulfilling their future profession can be, develop substantial a devotion to it. The practical work gives them the opportunity to do at least some of the core tasks done by their professional counterparts. All this occurs in an atmosphere that is essentially one of serious leisure, in that students can and do at times quit these training programs, giving substance to their basically uncoercive nature.

Hobbyists Become Crafts/Small Business People

Since today's trades invariably require formal schooling, many of the same recruitment and training arrangements prevail here as in the client-centered professions. What we will call "pre-apprentice" student hobbyists discover in their own courses and applied work a set of core tasks quite capable of engendering fulfillment and occupational devotion. Like their professional counterparts, it is rare that these hobbyists will have had as hobbyists any significant prior contact with their chosen trade. With both groups, the trade or profession for which the student is training is evaluated from an external vantage point by that person. From here it appears to offer interesting, fulfilling work as well as a decent living. So why not try it (assuming the usual financial and academic admission requirements can be met)?

People going into one of the many of the small businesses find career patterns similar to those who become enamored of one of the public-centered professions. That is, occupational devotees in small business often get started as pure hobbyists, the family farm being an exception to this observation. Thus, commercial genealogists, who seem to develop a taste for their core activity through earlier historical work on their own families, enter the business world from a pure hobbyist background, as do those in the artistic crafts, repair and restoration, and dealing in collectibles.

Volunteers Become Organizational Workers

Among the organizational volunteers are those who use their altruistic role to explore for work in a particular segment of the job market. Sometimes these "marginal volunteers" (Stebbins 2001d, 4–6) hope to find employment by this route, accomplished by gaining experience that will better their chances of getting work in that field or a related one. Sometimes they simply want to explore the nature of work there, and sometimes they believe that volunteer experience will look good on their resume. This less-than-pure volunteering is common practice these days, especially in the age bracket fifteen to twenty-four (Statistics Canada 2001, 37). Yet, even when people are operating under pressure and obligation to find some sort of work and who "volunteer" their services as part of their search for such work, there are those who manage to find an occupation worthy of their devotion.

On the other hand, pure organizational volunteers—those who serve primarily for the fulfillment derived from executing attractive core tasks—may be hired to fill a remunerative post in their organization that generates occupational devotion. One such post is volunteer coordinator; it includes recruiting volunteers and matching them according to their capabilities and interests with the volunteer needs of the organization. And some pure organizational volunteers learn at close range about the fulfilling aspects of certain kinds of professional work carried out in their organization, giving them impetus to seek the training they need for this new career. A number of social workers, registered nurses, and recreational specialists got started this way.

Prevalence of the Extensions

In common sense it is held that work and leisure are separate spheres. Yet, the foregoing shows the spheres to be more permeable than customarily thought. But how common are these bridges across the boundary separating the two institutions? Three of the types are uncommon: spillover leisure, contemplation as serious leisure, and occupation devotion. Why? Because all three have, as their point of departure, devotee work.

That is most people work so they may be paid. Most people work out of necessity, not out of profound love for the job and the set of deeply felt values that they realize there. Granted, some of these people derive certain agreeable, albeit comparatively superficial, rewards from the work they must do to support themselves, which may be its social life, the positive recognition that comes with being employed (as opposed to unemployed), and the fact that working helps the time pass. But none of this is nearly as appealing as finding deep fulfillment in the core activities that lie at the center of the occupation. This is what distinguishes the occupational devotee. Moreover, others who work out of necessity may even fail to find superficial rewards in their jobs, the regular pay check being the only substantial reason for staying with them. In short, devotee work is relatively rare, and so therefore are its extensions in leisure.

Not so, however, with interstitial leisure. It helps pass the time while at work, and in this capacity, is probably wide spread, especially in work not closely supervised. As for project-based leisure at work, it seems to be less common than the interstitial variety, if for no other reason than fewer opportunities exist to engage in the former. Yet, it undoubtedly serves the same function.

Effects of the Five Bridges

Working in leisure and finding leisure in work, when both are expressions of occupational devotion, because they are uncommon, may be difficult to justify in some respects. Who in the devotee's circle of friends, relatives, and working colleagues profoundly understands this person's passion for the core activities that are so attractive? In the typical case, the answer to this question is that very few of these people have this depth of understanding. Instead they entertain a more nuanced and complex view of devotees. That is they are seen as a "bit odd" or "not with it," because such people prefer work-like activity to popular culture and casual leisure, and yet, possibly looked on as "distinguished," because passionate and steady pursuit of excellence in a respectable line of work has led to extraordinary professional or communal recognition, if not both. Of course, interstitial and project-based leisure at work fail to generate this problem, though, in the eyes of the boss, too much of the first could spark concern over the worker's commitment to the job.

Yet, on the whole, the five bridges across the boundary separating work and leisure are good. Casual and project-based leisure at work give a momentary respite from concentration, thereby regenerating the worker for approximately the next hour on the job. Much of interstitial leisure can probably be conceived of as building bonds among those workers participating in it, although such leisure taken as gossip, while building bonds among some people, would also help undermine bonds with certain others. Extracurricular projects at work, when effectively seen as leisure, give the workers involved something special to look forward to. Furthermore, they, too, could be occasions for building closer ties with work colleagues.

As for the self-fulfillment that comes with occupational devotion and serious leisure, it is capable of producing in the individual an exceptional kind of personal contentment with life and lifestyle (Stebbins 2007a). The sometimes negative social relations that accompany these intense pursuits in leisure and at work are, at least for the participant, more than offset by the huge rewards experienced in them. Indeed, the so-called eccentricity of the devotees may even be for them a quiet badge of distinction, and one of which they are most proud.

Finding Balance

The popular locution "work/life balance" will in this book refer to "work/leisure/obligation balance," which describes better the issue of finding a workable distribution of activity in everyday life. The two goals in this section are to explore the nature of this tripartite balance

61

and to explain how the matter of balance can be regarded as one of leisure's first principles.

What does "balance" mean, when applied to everyday living? In common sense it seems to refer to "spending more time with family," having more leisure time ("getting a life"), gaining some measure of freedom from unpleasant obligations (escaping the "rat race"), and similar adaptive strategies. In the study of leisure the answer to this question is much more subtle: people may find balance across work, leisure, and obligation by crafting a lifestyle that encompasses these three and that is endowed with substantial appeal. Everyone who is working has some kind of lifestyle bridging these domains. But it is also true that many people have lifestyles they would sooner be rid of, which is a goal they believe is next to impossible to achieve. How, then, to generate an appealing, balanced lifestyle spanning the three domains? This would be Aristotle's good life, often reached when people abandon some major aspects of their present unappealing lifestyle.

In broadest terms, finding an appealing lifestyle hinges on discretionary time commitment. More particularly it hinges, in part, on committing more hours to the activities one likes most, while subtracting hours from those one likes less or flatly dislikes. Understandably, this balancing act is easiest to carry off in the domain of leisure, where by definition people stay away from unappealing activities. Even here, however, some activities are more difficult than others to abandon on a whim. So the young male can, at the last moment, tell his friends that the weekend "pub crawl" no longer excites him and that, from here on, they can continue their escapades without him. But the actress, having grown tired of community theater as performed in her city, can only comfortably announce that, next season, she will be unavailable for roles. She cannot, without great social cost, quit midway through preparation for an upcoming play in the present season her role in that play, for to do so would leave many associates in a lurch and spoil immensely their serious leisure.

So an appealing, balanced lifestyle may be reached, in part, by tinkering with the balance of leisure activities, spending more time in some while cutting back time spent in others. But, if the person suffering from an imbalance in lifestyle has little free time, then a solution to this problem must be found by redeploying commitments in the other two domains. In one sense, anyway, decisions about which activities to commit less time to in these areas of life are more subtle and difficult than in the domain of leisure. For the first two domains are loaded with obligations that may, at least at first glance, appear to be absolutely fixed.

Let us look first at work. The disagreeable obligatory requirements of the job are probably, in most instances, difficult to change. If you are a taxi driver, server in a restaurant, or packer in a warehouse and you hate driving cars, waiting on diners, or filling and taping boxes, you must face the fact that little hope exists for changing these core activities. These are central and immutable features (social conditions) of the taxi, warehousing, and restaurant industries. Nevertheless, there are some options. For instance, driving taxis and serving diners usually need not be done as full-time work. Given this option could the driver's or the server's household get along on a part-time wage? Two, if the answer to this question is no, might the breadwinner find a second part-time job loaded with fewer unpleasant obligations?

This brings up the thorny issue of the amount of money a person needs for an agreeable work–leisure–obligation lifestyle. The strategies presented next presume that people seeking an attractive balance in these three domains do not estimate their social value as individuals by "what they are worth," by the amount of wealth they have amassed. With such a goal scaling back on opportunities to make ever more money is out of the question. Yet, for most people, this is not their first option, while for those whose social value is measured exclusively in monetary terms, it is no option at all.

We have no scientific data on how many people in modern society estimate their social value primarily in pecuniary terms. Although I suspect that their number is far from negligible, I also suspect that those who estimate their worth in other ways are noticeably more common. When it comes to abandoning activities fraught with disagreeable obligations for activities blessed with agreeable ones or with no obligations whatsoever, this latter group has some choices. Put otherwise they may choose among some viable strategies.

Optimal Leisure Lifestyle

This subject was introduced in the preceding chapter under the heading of the temporal space of leisure. It has to do with how we allocate our time across the three domains. People searching for an OLL strive to get the best return they can from use of their free time. What they consider "best" is, of course, a matter of personal definition, and the quality of an OLL is predicated, in part, on a person's awareness of at least some of the great range of potentially available leisure possibilities. Thus, people know they have an OLL when, from their own reasonably wide knowledge of feasible serious, casual, and project-based leisure activities and associated costs and rewards, they can say they have enhanced their well-being by finding their best combination in two or three of the forms.

So people enjoying an OLL are usually conscious of other appealing casual, serious, and project-based leisure activities, but nonetheless sufficiently satisfied with their present set to resist abandoning them or adopting still others. Nonetheless this might well change in the future, as an activity loses its appeal, the person loses his or her ability to do it, or new activities gain attractiveness. From what I have observed in my own research, people with OLLs seem to sense that, at a given point in time, if they try to do too much, they will force a hectic routine on themselves, risk diluting their leisure, and thereby become unable to participate fully in what they are enamored of.

Conclusion: Leisure as Fulcrum for Work/Life Balance

A sixth distinctive principle of leisure emerges when leisure is viewed through the lenses of the other two domains. In other words it is primarily with reference to leisure that we try to reach a decent, if not optimal, balance between work, leisure, and obligation. Most people strive to find more leisure (as defined in this book), accomplishing this by reducing work and nonwork obligations. Certainly very few people would routinely cut back on leisure (or work) to take on more nonwork obligations. A few might, however, try to reduce either leisure or nonwork obligations, so as to be able to devote more time to their paying job, or jobs. The workaholic, as conventionally defined today, would be an example. Occupational devotees might do the same, but by the definition of leisure used here, they are trying to find time to engage in more leisure, in a serious pursuit.

So leisure may be seen as having still another unique property. It is the fulcrum on which life's optimal balance of activities turns. In searching for an OLL, people strive to lighten the distal ends of the lever, the spaces of disagreeable work or nonwork obligation, if not both, with the intention of shifting the weight toward the center, the fulcrum. When successful, the result is, in general, more leisure activity and less unpleasant activity.

Where does devotee work fit in the search for an OLL? Despite its reclassification in this book as a kind of serious pursuit, the first is still work. And, in a discussion of the work/life balance, it must therefore be considered separately. Occupational devotees may well seek to optimize their (other) leisure, even though there is sure to be less of it compared with many other kinds of workers. After all we find here a strong desire to go to work and to pursue there certain highly attractive core activities, an orientation that inevitably cuts into leisure time and, quite possibly, even some of the time set aside for meeting nonwork obligations. Thus, for this comparatively small group of fortunate souls, the possibility exists of having the best of both the world of work and that of leisure in what I have called (Stebbins 2009a, 66) an *optimal positive lifestyle* (OPL). The best in positiveness in life—defined as both an upbeat attitude toward life and a rewarding level of participation in leisure—that most people may strive for is an OLL, even while the occupational devotee has the opportunity to reach an even broader positive existence through an OPL.

Either way leisure, as discussed in this book, is at the center of the quest for the good life.

When people think of leisure in their lives, some of them think of it with reference to this quest. It is part of what leisure means to them. But I say "some" people because by no means everyone is looking for an OLL or OPL. Some people are too absorbed with their nondevotee work and nonwork obligations to do little more in their free time than "crash," often accomplished these days by watching television or surfing the Web. Others, among them certain retirees, have plenty of free time, but are unaware of the idea of the OLL or the OPL (some retirees continue on a part-time basis to work as occupational devotees). For finding either lifestyle requires the participant to engage consciously with available alternatives in the three spaces as the alternatives relate to that person's present and future. It is a question of personal agency, but people interested in the matter of balance must first know which actions to take to achieve it.

4

The Serious Leisure Perspective

The SLP can be described, in simplest terms, as the theoretic framework that synthesizes three main forms of leisure showing, at once, their distinctive features, similarities, and interrelationships (the SLP is discussed in detail in Stebbins [1992, 2001a, 2007a]). Additionally the Perspective (wherever Perspective appears as shorthand for SLP, to avoid confusion, the first letter will be capitalized) considers how the three forms—serious pursuits (serious leisure/devotee work), casual leisure, and project-based leisure—are shaped by various psychological, social, cultural, and historical conditions. Each form serves as a conceptual umbrella for a range of types of related activities. That the Perspective takes its name from the first of these should, in no way, suggest that it be regarded, in some abstract sense, as the most important or superior of the three. Rather the Perspective is so titled, simply because it got its start in the study of serious leisure; such leisure is, strictly from the standpoint of intellectual invention, the godfather of the other two. Furthermore, serious leisure has become the bench mark from which analyses of casual and project-based leisure have often been undertaken. So naming the Perspective after the first facilitates intellectual recognition; it keeps the idea in familiar territory for all concerned.

My research findings and theoretic musings over the past thirty-eight years have nevertheless evolved and coalesced into a typological map of the world of leisure (for a brief history of the Perspective, see the history page at http://www.soci.ucalgary.ca/seriousleisure, or for a longer version, see Stebbins [2007a, chap. 6]). That is, so far as known at present, all leisure (at least in Western society) can be classified according to one of the three forms and their several types and subtypes. More precisely the SLP offers a classification and explanation of all leisure activities and experiences, as these two are framed in the social

The Serious Leisure Perspective
(January 2011)

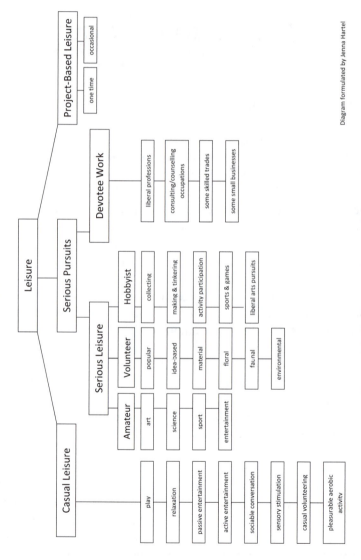

Diagram formulated by Jenna Hartel

Figure 4.1 The Serious Leisure Perspective

psychological, social, cultural, geographical, and historical conditions in which each activity and accompanying experience take place. Figure 4.1 portrays the typological structure of the Perspective.

Serious Pursuits

In Chapter 1 serious leisure and devotee work were placed under the heading of serious pursuits, as its two types. The present chapter further explains this classificatory change, from what was to this point in the history of the SLP a separation of the two as leisure and work, respectively. The justification for this change is simple: devotee work is essentially leisure. So we should call this spade a spade and explore it as part of the Perspective.

Serious Leisure

Serious leisure, one of the two types of serious pursuit, is the systematic pursuit of an amateur, hobbyist, or volunteer activity sufficiently substantial, interesting, and fulfilling for the participant to find a (leisure) career there acquiring and expressing a combination of its special skills, knowledge, and experience. I coined the term (Stebbins 1982) to express the way the people he interviewed and observed viewed the importance of these three kinds of activity in their everyday lives. The adjective "serious" (a word my research respondents often used) embodies such qualities as earnestness, sincerity, importance, and carefulness, rather than gravity, solemnity, joylessness, distress, and anxiety. Although the second set of terms occasionally describes serious leisure events, they are uncharacteristic of them and fail to nullify, or, in many cases, even dilute, the overall fulfillment gained by the participants. The idea of "career" in this definition follows sociological tradition, where careers are seen as available in all substantial, complex roles, including those in leisure. Finally, as we shall see shortly, serious leisure is distinct from casual leisure and project-based leisure.

Amateurs are found in art, science, sport, and entertainment, where they are invariably linked in a variety of ways with professional counterparts. The two can be distinguished descriptively in that the activity in question constitutes a livelihood for professionals but not amateurs. Furthermore, most professionals work full time at the activity, whereas all amateurs pursue it part time. The part-time professionals in art and entertainment complicate this picture; although they work part time, their work is judged by other professionals and by the amateurs as of professional quality. Amateurs and professionals are locked in and therefore defined by a system of relations linking them and their publics—the "professional-amateur-public system," or P-A-P system (discussed in more detail in Stebbins [2007a, 6–8], including Yoder's [1997] addition of the C-PC-AP system). But note here that enactment of the core activity by the professionals in a particular field, to influence amateurs there, must be sufficiently visible to those amateurs. If the amateurs, in general, have no idea of the prowess of their professional counterparts, the latter become irrelevant as role models, and the leisure side of the activity remains at a hobbyist level.

Hobbyists lack this professional alter ego, suggesting that, historically, all amateurs were hobbyists before their fields professionalized. Both types are drawn to their leisure pursuits significantly more by self-interest than by altruism, whereas volunteers engage in activities requiring a more or less equal blend of these two motives. Hobbyists may be classified in five types: collectors, makers and tinkerers, noncompetitive activity participants (e.g., fishing, hiking, orienteering), hobbyist sports and games (e.g., ultimate Frisbee, croquet, gin rummy), and the liberal arts hobbies.

The liberal arts hobbyists are enamored of the systematic acquisition of knowledge for its own sake. Many of them accomplish this by reading voraciously in a field of art, sport, cuisine, language, culture, history, science, philosophy, politics, or literature (Stebbins 1994). But some of them go beyond this to expand their knowledge still further through cultural tourism, documentary videos, television programs, and similar resources. Although the matter has yet to be studied through research, it is theoretically possible to separate buffs from consumers in the liberal arts hobbies of sport, cuisine, and the fine and entertainment arts. Some people—call them *consumers*—more or less uncritically consume restaurant fare, sports events, or displays of art (concerts, shows, exhibitions) as pure entertainment and sensory stimulation (casual leisure), whereas others—call them *buffs*—participate in these same situations as more or less knowledgeable experts, as serious leisure (for more on this distinction, see Stebbins [2002, chap. 5]). The ever rarer Renaissance man of our day may also be classified here, even though such people avoid specializing in one field of learning to acquire, instead, a somewhat more superficial knowledge of a variety of fields. Being broadly well-read is a (liberal arts) hobby of its own.

What have been referred to as "the nature-challenge activities" (Davidson and Stebbins 2011) fall primarily under the hobbyist heading of noncompetitive, rule-based activity participation. True, actual competitions are sometimes held in, for instance, snowboarding, kayaking, and mountain biking (e.g., fastest time over a particular course), but mostly beating nature is thrill enough. Moreover, other nature hobbies exist, which are also challenging, but in very different ways. Some, most notably fishing and hunting, in essence exploit the natural environment. Still others center on appreciation of the outdoors, among them hiking, backpacking, bird watching, and horseback riding.

Smith, Stebbins, and Dover (2006, 239–40) define *volunteer*— whether economic or volitional—as someone who performs, even for a short period of time, volunteer work in either an informal or a formal setting. It is through volunteer work that this person provides a service or benefit to one or more individuals (they must be outside that person's family), usually receiving no pay, even though people serving in volunteer programs are sometimes compensated for out-of-pocket expenses. Moreover, in the field of nonprofit studies, since no volunteer work is involved, giving (of, say, blood, money, clothing), as an altruistic act, is not considered volunteering. Meanwhile, in the typical case, volunteers who are altruistically providing a service or benefit to others are themselves also benefiting from various rewards experienced during this process (e.g., pleasant social interaction, self-enriching experiences, sense of contributing to nonprofit group success). In other words, volunteering is motivated by two basic attitudes: altruism *and* self-interest.

The conception of volunteering that squares best with the idea of leisure revolves, in significant part, around a central subjective motivational question: it must be determined whether volunteers feel they are engaging in an enjoyable (casual leisure), fulfilling (serious leisure), or enjoyable or fulfilling (project-based leisure) core activity that they have had the option to accept or reject on their own terms. A key element in the leisure conception of volunteering is the felt absence of coercion, moral or otherwise, to participate in the volunteer activity (Stebbins 1996c), an element that, in "marginal volunteering" (Stebbins 2001d) may be experienced in degrees, as more or less coercive. The reigning conception of volunteering in nonprofit sector research is not that of volunteering as leisure, but rather volunteering as unpaid work. The first—an *economic* conception—defines volunteering as the absence of payment as livelihood, whether in money or in kind. This definition, for the most part, leaves unanswered the messy question of motivation so crucial to the second, positive sociological, definition, which is a *volitional* conception.

Volitionally speaking, volunteer activities are motivated, in part, by one of six types of interest: interest in activities involving (1) people, (2) ideas, (3) things, (4) flora, (5) fauna, or (6) the natural environment (Stebbins 2007b). Each type, or combination of types, offers its volunteers an opportunity to pursue, through an altruistic activity, a particular kind of interest. Thus, volunteers interested in working with certain ideas are attracted to idea-based volunteering, while those interested in certain kinds of animals are attracted to faunal volunteering. Interest forms the first dimension of a typology of volunteers and volunteering.

But, since volunteers and volunteering cannot be explained by interest alone, a second dimension is needed. This is supplied by the SLP and its three forms. This Perspective, as already noted, sets out the motivational and contextual (sociocultural, historical) foundation of the three. The intersections of these two dimensions produce eighteen types of volunteers and volunteering, exemplified in idea-based serious leisure volunteers, material casual leisure volunteering (working with things), and environmental project-based volunteering (see Table 4.1).

Six Qualities

Serious leisure is further defined by six distinctive qualities, qualities uniformly found among its amateurs, hobbyists, and volunteers. One is the occasional need to *persevere*. Participants who want to continue experiencing the same level of fulfillment in the activity have

Table 4.1 Types of Volunteers and Volunteering

Leisure Interest	Type of Volunteer		
	Serious Leisure (SL)	Casual Leisure (CL)	Project-Based Leisure (PBL)
Popular	SL Popular	CL Popular	PBL Popular
Idea-Based	SL Idea-Based	CL Idea-Based	PBL Idea-Based
Material	SL Material	CL Material	PBL Material
Floral	SL Floral	CL Floral	PBL Floral
Faunal	SL Faunal	CL Faunal	PBL Faunal
Environmental	SL Environmental	CL Environmental	PBL Environmental

to meet certain challenges from time to time. Thus, musicians must practice assiduously to master difficult musical passages, baseball players must throw repeatedly to perfect favorite pitches, and volunteers must search their imaginations for new approaches with which to help children with reading problems. It happens in all three types of serious leisure that deepest fulfillment sometimes comes at the end of the activity rather than during it, from sticking with it through thick and thin, from conquering adversity.

Another quality distinguishing all three types of serious leisure is the opportunity to follow a (leisure) *career* in the endeavor, a career shaped by its own special contingencies, turning points, and stages of achievement and involvement. A career that, in some fields notably certain arts and sports may nevertheless include decline. Moreover, most, if not all, careers here owe their existence to a third quality: serious leisure participants make significant personal *effort* using their specially acquired knowledge, training, or skill and, indeed at times, all three. Careers for serious leisure participants unfold along lines of their efforts to achieve, for instance, a high level of showmanship, athletic prowess, or scientific knowledge or to accumulate formative experiences in a volunteer role.

Serious leisure is further distinguished by several *durable benefits*, or tangible, salutary outcomes such activity for its participants. They include self-actualization, self-enrichment, self-expression, regeneration or renewal of self, feelings of accomplishment, enhancement of self-image, social interaction and sense of belonging, and lasting physical products of the activity (e.g., a painting, scientific paper, piece of furniture). A further benefit—self-gratification, or pure fun, which is by far the most evanescent benefit in this list—is also enjoyed by casual leisure participants. The possibility of realizing such benefits constitutes a powerful goal in serious leisure.

Fifth, serious leisure is distinguished by a unique *ethos* that emerges in parallel with each expression of it. An ethos is the spirit of the community of serious leisure participants, as manifested in shared attitudes, practices, values, beliefs, goals, and so on. The social world of the participants is the organizational milieu in which the associated ethos—at bottom a cultural formation—is expressed (as attitudes, beliefs, values) or realized (as practices, goals). According to David Unruh (1979, 1980), every social world has its characteristic groups, events, routines, practices, and organizations. It is held together, to an important degree, by semiformal, or mediated, communication. In other words, in the typical case, social worlds are neither heavily bureaucratized nor substantially organized through intense face-to-face interaction. Rather, communication is commonly mediated by newsletters, posted notices, telephone messages, mass mailings, radio and television announcements, and similar means. Unruh (1980, 277) says of the social world that it

> must be seen as a unit of social organization which is diffuse and amorphous in character. Generally larger than groups or organizations, social worlds are not necessarily defined by formal boundaries, membership lists, or spatial territory.... A social world must be seen as an internally recognizable constellation of actors, organizations, events, and practices which have coalesced into a perceived sphere of interest and involvement for participants. Characteristically, a social world lacks a powerful centralized authority structure and is delimited by...effective communication and not territory nor formal group membership.

The social world is a diffuse, amorphous entity to be sure, but nevertheless one of great importance in the impersonal, segmented life of the modern urban community. Its importance is further amplified by a parallel element of the special ethos, which is missing from Unruh's conception, namely that such worlds are also constituted of a rich subculture. One function of this subculture is to inter-relate the many components of this diffuse and amorphous entity. In other words, there is associated with each social world a set of special norms, values, beliefs, styles, moral principles, performance standards, and similar shared representations.

Every social world contains four types of members: strangers, tourists, regulars, and insiders (Unruh 1979, 1980). The strangers are intermediaries who normally participate little in the leisure activity itself, but who nonetheless do something important to make it possible, for example, by managing municipal parks (in amateur baseball), minting coins (in hobbyist coin collecting), and organizing the work of teachers' aids (in career volunteering). Tourists are temporary participants in a social world; they have come on the scene momentarily for entertainment, diversion, or profit. Most amateur and hobbyist activities have publics of some kind, which are, at bottom, constituted of tourists. The clients of many volunteers can be similarly classified. The regulars routinely participate in the social world; in serious leisure, they are the amateurs, hobbyists, and volunteers themselves. The insiders are those among them who show exceptional devotion to the social world they share, to maintaining it, to advancing it. In the SLP, such people are analyzed according to an involvement scale as either "core devotees" or "moderate devotees" and contrasted with "participants," or regulars (Siegenthaler and O'Dell 2003; Stebbins 2007a, 20–21).

The sixth quality—participants in serious leisure tend to identify strongly with their chosen pursuits—springs from the presence of the other five distinctive qualities. In contrast, most casual leisure, although not usually humiliating or despicable, is nonetheless too fleeting, mundane, and commonplace to become the basis for a distinctive *identity* for most people.

Rewards, Costs, and Motivation

Furthermore, certain rewards and costs come with pursuing a hobbyist, amateur, or volunteer activity. Both implicitly and explicitly much of serious leisure theory rests on the following assumption: to understand the meaning of such leisure for those who pursue it is in significant part to understand their motivation for the pursuit. Moreover, one fruitful approach to understanding the motives that lead to serious leisure participation is to study them through the eyes of the participants who, past studies reveal (e.g., Arai and Pedlar 1997; Stebbins 1992, chap. 6), see it as a mix of offsetting costs and rewards experienced in the central activity. The rewards of this activity tend to outweigh the costs, however, the result being that the participants usually find a high level of personal fulfillment in them.

In these studies the participant's leisure fulfillment has been found to stem from a constellation of particular rewards gained from the activity, be it boxing, ice climbing, or giving dance lessons to the elderly. Furthermore, the rewards are not only fulfilling in themselves, but also fulfilling as counterweights to the costs encountered in the activity. That is, every serious leisure activity contains its own combination of tensions, dislikes, and disappointments, which each participant must confront in some way. For instance, an amateur football player may not always like attending daily practices, being bested occasionally by more junior players when there, and being required to sit on the sidelines from time to time while others get experience at his position. Yet, he may still regard this activity as highly fulfilling—as (serious) leisure—because it also offers certain powerful rewards.

Put more precisely, then, the drive to find fulfillment in serious leisure is the drive to experience the rewards of a given leisure activity, such that its costs are seen by the participant as more or less insignificant by comparison. This is at once the meaning of the activity for the participant and his or her motivation for engaging in it. It is this motivational sense of the concept of reward that distinguishes it from the idea of durable benefit set out earlier, a concept that, as I said, emphasizes outcomes rather than antecedent conditions. Nonetheless, the two ideas constitute two sides of the same social psychological coin.

The rewards of a serious leisure pursuit are the more or less routine values that attract and hold its enthusiasts. Every serious leisure career both frames and is framed by the continuous search for these rewards, a search that takes months, and in some fields years, before the participant consistently finds deep satisfaction in his or her amateur, hobbyist, or volunteer role. Ten rewards have so far emerged in the course of the various exploratory studies of amateurs, hobbyists, and career volunteers. As the following list shows, the rewards are predominantly personal.

Personal rewards
1. Personal enrichment (cherished experiences)
2. Self-actualization (developing skills, abilities, knowledge)
3. Self-expression (expressing skills, abilities, knowledge already developed)
4. Self-image (known to others as a particular kind of serious leisure participant)
5. Self-gratification (combination of superficial enjoyment and deep fulfillment)
6. Re-creation (regeneration) of oneself through serious leisure after a day's work
7. Financial return (from a serious leisure activity)

Social rewards
8. Social attraction (associating with other serious leisure participants, with clients as a volunteer, participating in the social world of the activity)
9. Group accomplishment (group effort in accomplishing a serious leisure project; senses of helping, being needed, being altruistic)
10. Contribution to the maintenance and development of the group (including senses of helping, being needed, being altruistic in making the contribution)

This brief discussion shows that some positive psychological states may be founded, to some extent, on particular negative, often note-worthy, conditions (e.g., tennis elbow, frostbite [cross-country skiing], stage fright, and frustration [in acquiring a collectable, learning a part]). Such conditions can make the senses of achievement and self-fulfill-ment even more pronounced as the enthusiast manages to conquer adversity. The broader lesson here is that, to understand motivation in serious leisure, we must always examine costs and rewards in their relationship to each other.

Serious leisure experiences also have a negative side, which must always be assessed. Accordingly, I have always asked my respondents to discuss the costs they face in their serious leisure. But so far, it has been impossible to develop a general list of them, as has been done for rewards, since the costs tend to be highly specific to each serious leisure activity. Thus, each activity I have studied to date has been found to have its own constellation of costs, but as the respondents see them, they are invariably and heavily outweighed in importance by the rewards of the activity. In general terms, the costs discovered to date may be classified as disappointments, dislikes, or tensions. Nonetheless, all research on serious leisure considered, its costs are not nearly as commonly examined as its rewards, leaving thus a gap in our understanding that must be filled.

The costs of leisure may also be seen as one type of leisure constraint. Leisure constraints, are "factors that limit people's participation in leisure activities, use of services, and satisfaction or enjoyment of current activities" (Scott 2003, 75). Costs certainly dilute the satisfac-tion or enjoyment participants experience in pursuing certain leisure activities, even if, in their interpretation of them, those participants find such costs, or constraints, overridden by the powerful rewards also found there.

Thrills and Psychological Flow

Thrills are part of this reward system. *Thrills*, or high points, are the sharply exciting events and occasions that stand out in the minds of those who pursue a kind of serious leisure or devotee work. In general, they tend to be associated with the rewards of self-enrichment and, to a lesser extent, those of self-actualization and self-expression. That is, thrills in serious leisure and devotee work may be seen as situated manifestations of certain more abstract rewards; they are what par-ticipants in some fields seek as concrete expressions of the rewards they find there. They are important, in substantial part, because they motivate the participant to stick with the pursuit in hope of finding similar experiences again and again and because they demonstrate that diligence and commitment may pay off. Because thrills, as defined here, are based on a certain level of mastery of a core activity, they know no equivalent in casual leisure. The thrill of a roller coaster ride is qualitatively different from a successful descent down a roaring rapids in a kayak where the boater has the experience, knowledge, and skill to accomplish this.

Over the years I have identified a number of thrills that come with the serious leisure activities I studied. These thrills are exceptional instances of the *flow* experience. Thus, although the idea of flow originated with the work of Mihalyi Csikszentmihalyi (1990), and has therefore an intellectual history quite separate from that of serious leisure, it does nevertheless happen, depending on the activity, that it is a key motivational force there (Stebbins 2010a). What then is flow?

The intensity with which some participants approach their leisure suggests that, there, they may at times be in psychological flow. Flow, a form of optimal experience, is possibly the most widely discussed and studied generic intrinsic reward in the psychology of work and leisure. Although many types of work and leisure generate little or no flow for their participants, those that do are found primarily in the serious pursuits of devotee work and serious leisure. Still it appears that each serious pursuit capable of producing flow does so in terms unique to it. And it follows that each of these activities, especially their core activities, must be carefully studied to discover the properties contributing to the distinctive flow experience it offers.

In his theory of optimal experience, Csikszentmihalyi (1990, 3–5, 54) describes and explains the psychological foundation of the many flow activities in work and leisure, as exemplified in chess, dancing, surgery, and rock climbing. Flow is "autotelic" experience, or the sensation that comes with the actual enacting of intrinsically rewarding activity. Over the years Csikszentmihalyi (1990, 49–67) has identified and explored eight components of this experience. It is easy to see how this quality of complex core activity, when present, is sufficiently rewarding and, it follows, highly valued to endow it with many of the qualities of serious leisure, thereby rendering the two, at the motivational level, inseparable in several ways. And this holds even though most people tend to think of work and leisure as vastly different. The eight components are

1. sense of competence in executing the activity;
2. requirement of concentration;
3. clarity of goals of the activity;
4. immediate feedback from the activity;
5. sense of deep, focused involvement in the activity;
6. sense of control in completing the activity;
7. loss of self-consciousness during the activity;
8. sense of time is truncated during the activity.

These components are self-evident, except possibly for the first and the sixth. With reference to the first, flow fails to develop when the activity is either too easy or too difficult; to experience flow the participant must feel capable of performing a moderately challenging activity. The sixth component refers to the perceived degree of control the participant has over execution of the activity. This is not a matter of personal competence; rather it is one of degree of maneuverability in the fact of uncontrollable external forces, a condition well illustrated in situations faced by the mountain hobbyists mentioned above, as when the water level suddenly rises on the river or an unpredicted snowstorm results in a whiteout on a mountain snowboard slope.

Viewed from the SLP, psychological flow tends to be associated with the rewards of self-enrichment and, to a lesser extent, those of self-actualization and self-expression. Also to be considered part of the Perspective as well as part of flow theory are the pre and postflow phases of flow, recently examined by Elkington (2010). These were discussed in Chapter 1.

Costs, Uncontrollability, and Marginality

From the earlier statement about costs and rewards, it is evident why the desire to participate in the core amateur, hobbyist, or volunteer activity can become for some participants some of the time significantly *uncontrollable*. This is because it engenders in its practitioners the desire to engage in the activity beyond the time or the money (if not both) available for it. As a professional violinist once counseled his daughter, "Rachel, never marry an amateur violinist! He will want to play quartets all night" (from Bowen 1935, 93). There seems to be an almost universal desire to upgrade: to own a better set of golf clubs, buy a more powerful telescope, take more dance lessons perhaps from a renowned (and consequently more expensive) professional, and so forth. The same applies to hobbyist and volunteer pursuits.

Chances are therefore good that some serious leisure enthusiasts will be eager to spend more time at and money on the core activity than is likely to be countenanced by certain significant others who also make demands on that time and money. The latter may soon come to the interpretation that the enthusiast is more enamored of the core leisure activity than of, say, the partner or spouse. Charges of selfishness may, then, not be long off. I found in my research on serious leisure that attractive activity and selfishness are natural partners (Stebbins 2007a, 74–75). Whereas some casual leisure and even project-based leisure can also be uncontrollable, the marginality hypothesis (stated below) implies that such a proclivity is generally significantly stronger among serious leisure participants.

Uncontrollable or not serious leisure activities, given their intense appeal, can also be viewed as behavioral expressions of the participants' *central life interests* in those activities. In his book by the same title, Robert Dubin (1992) defines this interest as that portion of a person's total life in which energies are invested in both physical/intellectual activities and in positive emotional states." Sociologically, a central life interest is often associated with a major role in life. And since they can only emerge from positive emotional states, obsessive and compulsive activities can never become central life interests.

Finally, I have argued over the years that amateurs, and sometimes even the activities they pursue, are marginal in society, for amateurs are neither dabblers (casual leisure) nor professionals (see Stebbins 2007a, 18). Moreover, studies of hobbyists and career volunteers show that they and some of their activities are just as marginal and for many of the same reasons. Several properties of serious leisure give substance to these observations. One, although seemingly illogical according to common sense, is that serious leisure is characterized empirically by an important degree of positive commitment to a pursuit. This commitment is measured, among other ways, by the sizeable investments of time and energy in the leisure made by its devotees and participants. Two, serious leisure is pursued with noticeable intentness, with such passion that Erving Goffman (1963, 144–45) once branded amateurs and hobbyists as the "quietly disaffiliated." People with such orientations toward their leisure are marginal compared with people who go in for the ever-popular forms of much of casual leisure.

Career

Leisure career, introduced earlier as a central component of the definition of serious leisure and as one of its six distinguishing qualities, is important enough as a concept in this exposition of the basics of this form of leisure to warrant still further discussion. One reason for this special treatment is that a person's sense of the unfolding of his or her career in any complex role, leisure roles included, can be, at times, a powerful motive to act there. For example, a woman who knits a sweater that a friend praises highly is likely to feel some sense of her own abilities in this hobby and be motivated to continue in it, possibly trying more complicated patterns. Athletes who win awards for excellence in their sport can get from this a similar jolt of enthusiasm for participation there.

Exploratory research on careers in serious leisure has so far proceeded from a broad, rather loose definition: a leisure career is the typical course, or passage, of a type of amateur, hobbyist, or volunteer that carries the person into and through a leisure role and possibly into and through a work role. The essence of any career, whether in work, leisure, or elsewhere, lies in the temporal continuity of the activities associated with it. Moreover, we are accustomed to thinking of this continuity as one of accumulating rewards and prestige, as progress along these lines from some starting point, even though continuity may also include career retrogression. In the worlds of sport and entertainment, for instance, athletes and artists may reach performance peaks early on, after which the prestige and rewards diminish as the limelight shifts to younger, sometimes more capable practitioners.

Career continuity may occur predominantly within, between, or outside organizations. Careers in organizations such as a community orchestra or hobbyist association only rarely involve the challenge of the "bureaucratic crawl," to use the imagery of C. Wright Mills. In other words, little or no hierarchy exists for them to climb. Nevertheless, the amateur or hobbyist still gains a profound sense of continuity, and hence career, from his or her more or less steady development as a skilled, experienced, and knowledgeable participant in a particular form of serious leisure and from the deepening fulfillment that accompanies this kind of personal growth. Moreover, some volunteer careers may be intraorganizational, a good example of this being available in the world of the barbershop singer (Stebbins 1996a, chap. 3).

Still, many amateurs and volunteers as well as some hobbyists have careers that bridge two or more organizations. For them, career continuity stems from their growing reputations as skilled, knowledgeable practitioners and, based on this image, from finding increasingly better leisure opportunities available through various outlets (as in different teams, orchestras, organizations, tournaments, exhibitions, journals, conferences, contests, shows, and the like). Meanwhile, still other amateurs and hobbyists who pursue noncollective lines of leisure (e.g., tennis, painting, clowning, golf, entertainment magic) are free of even this marginal affiliation with an organization. The extraorganizational career of the informal volunteer, the forever willing and sometimes highly skilled and knowledgeable helper of friends and neighbors is of this third type.

Serious leisure participants who stick with their activities eventually pass through four, possibly five career stages: beginning, development, establishment, maintenance, and decline. But the boundaries separating these stages are imprecise, for as the condition of continuity suggests, the participant passes largely imperceptibly from one to the next. The beginning lasts as long as is necessary for interest in the activity to take root. Development begins when the interest has taken root and its pursuit becomes more or less routine and systematic. Serious leisure participants advance to the establishment stage once they have moved beyond the requirement of having to learn the basics of their activity. During the maintenance stage, the leisure career is in full bloom; here participants are now able to enjoy to the utmost their pursuit of it, the uncertainties of getting established having been, for the most part, put behind them. By no means all serious leisure participants face decline, but those who do, may experience it because of deteriorating mental or physical skills. And it appears to happen—though I know not how often—that the bloom simply falls off the rose; that leisure participants sometimes reach a point of diminishing returns in the activity, getting out of it all they believe is available for them. Now it is less fulfilling, perhaps on occasion even boring. Now it is time to search for a new activity. A more detailed description of the career framework and its five stages, along with empirical support for them, is available elsewhere (Heuser 2005; Stebbins 1992, chap. 5).

Although this can vary according to where in their careers participants in serious leisure are, I have observed over the years that, at any one point time, they can be classified as either *devotees* or *participants*. The devotees are highly dedicated to their pursuits, whereas the participants are only moderately interested in it, albeit significantly more so than dabblers. Participants typically greatly outnumber devotees. Along this dimension devotees and participants are operationally distinguished primarily by the different amounts of time they commit to their hobby, as manifested in engaging in the core activity, training or preparing for it, reading about it, and the like.

This is, however, a rather crude scale of intensity of involvement in a serious leisure activity, a weakness not missed by Siegenthaler and O'Dell (2003, 51). Their findings from a study of older golfers and successful aging revealed that data on leisure career are more effectively considered according to three types, labeled by them as "social," "moderate," and "core devotee." The moderate is equivalent to the participant, whereas the social player falls into a class of players who are more skilled and involved than dabblers but less skilled and involved than the moderates (participants). To keep terminology consistent with past theory and research and the generality of the earlier two terms, I suggest we calibrate this new, more detailed, involvement scale with appropriate, new terms: *participant, moderate devotee*, and *core devotee*.

Recreational Specialization

Recreational specialization is both process and product. As process it refers to a progressive narrowing of interests within a complex leisure activity; "a continuum of behavior from the general to the particular" (Bryan 1977, 175). Viewed as an aspect of serious leisure, specialization can be seen as part of the leisure career experienced in those complex activities that offer participants who want to focus their interests an opportunity to specialize (Stebbins 2005e). In particular, when specialization occurs, it unfolds as a process within the development or establishment stage, possibly spanning the two (of the five-stage sequence of beginning, development, establishment, maintenance, and decline), or should the participant change specialties, it unfolds within the maintenance stage. In career terminology, developing a specialty is a career turning point.

Devotee Work

The subject of devotee work and occupational devotion was partially covered in Chapters 1 and 3. There it was observed that occupational devotees feel a powerful devotion, or strong, positive attachment, to a form of self-enhancing work. In such work the sense of achievement is high and the core activity endowed with such intense appeal that the line between this work and leisure is virtually erased. Further, it is by way of the core activity of their work that devotees realize a unique combination of, what are for them, strongly seated cultural values (Williams 2000, 146): success, achievement, freedom of action, individual personality, and activity (being involved in something). Other categories of workers may also be animated by some, even all, of these values, but fail for various reasons to realize them in gainful employment.

Occupational devotees turn up chiefly, though not exclusively, in four areas of the economy, providing their work there is, at most, only lightly bureaucratized: certain small businesses, the skilled trades, the consulting and counseling occupations, and the public- and client-centered professions. Public-centered professions are found in the arts, sports, scientific, and entertainment fields, while those that are client-centered abound in such fields as law, teaching, accounting, and medicine (Stebbins 1992, 22). It is assumed in all this that the work and its core activity to which people become devoted carries with it a respectable personal and social identity within their reference groups, since it would be difficult, if not impossible, to be devoted to work that those groups regarded with scorn. Still, positive identification with the job is not a defining condition of occupational devotion, since such identification can develop for other reasons, including high salary, prestigious employer, and advanced educational qualifications.

The fact of devotee work for some people and its possibility for others signals that work, as one of life's domains, may be highly positive. Granted, most workers are not fortunate enough to find such work. For those who do find it, the work meets six criteria (Stebbins 2004a, 9). To generate occupational devotion:

1. The valued core activity must be profound; to perform it acceptability requires substantial skill, knowledge, or experience or a combination of two or three of these.
2. The core must offer significant variety.
3. The core must also offer significant opportunity for creative or innovative work, as a valued expression of individual personality. The adjectives "creative" and "innovative" stress that the undertaking results in something new or different, showing imagination and application of routine skill or knowledge. That is, boredom is likely to develop only after the onset of fatigue experienced from long hours on the job, a point at which significant creativity and innovation are no longer possible.

4. The would-be devotee must have reasonable control over the amount and disposition of time put into the occupation (the value of freedom of action), such that he can prevent it from becoming a burden. Medium and large bureaucracies have tended to subvert this criterion. For, in interest of the survival and development of their organization, managers have felt they must deny their nonunionized employees this freedom, and force them to accept stiff deadlines and heavy workloads. But no activity, be it leisure or work, is so appealing that it invites unlimited participation during all waking hours.

5. The would-be devotee must have both an aptitude and a taste for the work in question. This is, in part, a case of one man's meat being another man's poison. John finds great fulfillment in being a physician, an occupation that holds little appeal for Jane who, instead, adores being a lawyer (work John finds unappealing).

6. The devotees must work in a physical and social milieu that encourages them to pursue often and without significant constraint the core activity. This includes avoidance of excessive paperwork, caseloads, class sizes, market demands, and the like.

Sounds ideal, if not idealistic, but in fact occupations and work roles exist that meet these criteria. In today's climate of occupational deskilling, over-bureaucratization, and similar impediments to fulfilling core activity at work, many people find it difficult to locate or arrange devotee employment. The six criteria just listed also characterize serious leisure, giving further substance to the claim put forward here that such leisure and devotee work occupy a great deal of common ground. Together they constitute the class of serious pursuits.

Casual Leisure

Casual leisure is immediately intrinsically rewarding, relatively short-lived pleasurable activity requiring little or no special training to enjoy it. It is fundamentally hedonic, pursued for its significant level of pure enjoyment, or pleasure. The term was coined by the author in the first conceptual statement about serious leisure (Stebbins 1982), which at the time, depicted its casual counterpart as all activity not classifiable as serious (project-based leisure has since been added as a third form, see next section). Casual leisure is considerably less substantial than serious leisure, and offers no career of the sort found in the latter.

Its types—there are eight (see Figure 4.1)—include *play* (including dabbling), relaxation (e.g., sitting, napping, strolling), *passive entertainment* (e.g., popular TV, books, recorded music), *active entertainment* (e.g., games of chance, party games), *sociable conversation* (e.g., gossiping, joking, talking about the weather), *sensory stimulation* (e.g., sex, eating, drinking, sight-seeing), and *casual volunteering* (as opposed to serious leisure, or career, volunteering). Casual volunteering includes handing out leaflets, stuffing envelopes, and collecting money door-to-door. Note that dabbling (as play) may occur in the same genre of activity pursued by amateurs, hobbyists, and career volunteers. The preceding section was designed, in part, to conceptually separate dabblers from this trio of leisure participants, thereby enabling the reader to interpret with sophistication references to, for example, "amateurish" activity (e.g., *The cult of the amateur* by Andrew Keen [2007]).

The last and newest type of casual leisure—*pleasurable aerobic activity*—refers to physical activities that require effort sufficient to cause marked increase in respiration and heart rate. As applied here the term "aerobic activity" is broad in scope, encompassing all activity that calls for such effort, which to be sure, includes the routines pursued collectively in (narrowly conceived of) aerobics classes and those pursued individually by way of televised or video-taped programs of aerobics (Stebbins 2004b). Yet, as with its passive and active cousins in entertainment, pleasurable aerobic activity is basically casual leisure. That is, to do such activity requires little more than minimal skill, knowledge, or experience. Examples include the game of the Hash House Harriers (a type of treasure hunt in the outdoors), kickball (described in The *Economist* [2005] as a cross between soccer and baseball), "exergames" for children (a video game played on a dance floor, Gerson [2010]), and such children's pastimes as hide-and-seek.

People seem to pursue the different types of casual leisure in combinations of two and three at least as often as they pursue them separately. For instance, every type can be relaxing, producing in this fashion play-relaxation, passive entertainment-relaxation, and so on. Various combinations of play and sensory stimulation are also possible, as in experimenting, in deviant or nondeviant ways, with drug use, sexual activity, and thrill seeking through movement. Additionally, sociable conversation accompanies some sessions of sensory stimulation (e.g., recreational drug use, curiosity seeking, displays of beauty) as well as some sessions of relaxation and active and passive entertainment, although such conversation normally tends to be rather truncated in the latter two.

This brief review of the types of casual leisure reveals that they share at least one central property: all are hedonic. More precisely, all produce a significant level of pure pleasure, or enjoyment, for those participating in them. In broad, colloquial language, casual leisure could serve as the scientific term for the practice of doing what comes naturally. Yet, paradoxically, this leisure is by no means wholly frivolous, for we shall see shortly that some clear benefits come from pursuing it. Moreover, unlike the evanescent hedonic property of casual leisure itself, its benefits are enduring, a property that makes them worthy of extended analysis in their own right.

It follows that terms such as "pleasure" and "enjoyment" are the more appropriate descriptors of the rewards of casual leisure in contrast to terms such as "fulfillment" and "rewardingness," which best describe the rewards gained in serious leisure. At least the serious leisure participants interviewed by the author were inclined to describe their involvements as fulfilling or rewarding rather than pleasurable or enjoyable. Still, overlap exists, for both casual and serious leisure offer the hedonic reward of self-gratification (see reward number 5). The activity is fun to do, even if the fun component is considerably more prominent in casual leisure than in its serious counterpart.

Notwithstanding its hedonic nature, casual leisure is by no means wholly inconsequential, for some clear costs and benefits accrue from pursuing it. Moreover, in contrast to the evanescent hedonic property of casual leisure itself, these costs and benefits are enduring. The benefits include serendipitous creativity and discovery in play, regeneration from earlier intense activity, and development and maintenance of interpersonal relationships (Stebbins 2007a, 41–43). Some of its costs root in excessive casual leisure or lack of variety as manifested in boredom or lack of time for leisure activities that contribute to self through acquisition of skills, knowledge, and experience (i.e., serious leisure). Moreover, casual leisure is alone unlikely to produce a distinctive leisure identity.

Moreover, my own observations of casual leisure suggest that hedonism, or self-gratification, although it is a principal reward here, must still share the stage with one or two other rewards. Thus, any type of casual leisure, like any type of serious leisure, can also help *re-create*, or regenerate, its participants following a lengthy stint of obligatory activity. Furthermore, some forms of casual and serious leisure offer the reward of *social attraction*, the appeal of being with other people while participating in a common activity. Nevertheless, even though some casual and serious leisure participants share certain rewards, research on this question will likely show that these two types experience them in sharply different ways. For example, the social attraction of belonging to a barbershop chorus or a company of actors with all its specialized shoptalk diverges considerably from that of belonging to a group of people playing a party game or taking a boat tour where such talk is highly unlikely to occur.

Benefits of Casual Leisure

We have so far been able to identify five benefits, or outcomes, of casual leisure. But since this is a preliminary list—they first attempt at making one—it is certainly possible that future research and theorizing could add to it.

One lasting benefit of casual leisure is the creativity and discovery it sometimes engenders. Serendipity, "the quintessential form of informal experimentation, accidental discovery, and spontaneous invention" (Stebbins 2001b), usually underlies these two processes, suggesting that serendipity and casual leisure are at times closely aligned. In casual leisure, as elsewhere, serendipity can lead to highly varied results, including a new understanding of a home gadget or government policy, a sudden realization that a particular plant or bird exists in the neighborhood, or a different way of making artistic sounds on a musical instrument. Such creativity or discovery is unintended, however, and is therefore accidental. Moreover, it is not ordinarily the result of a problem-solving orientation of people taking part in casual leisure, since most of the time at least, they have little interest in trying to solve problems while engaging in this kind of activity. Usually problems for which solutions must be found emerge at work, while meeting nonwork obligations, or during serious leisure.

Another benefit springs from what has come to be known as *edutainment*. Nahrstedt (2000) holds that this benefit of casual leisure comes with participating in such mass entertainment as watching films and television programs, listening to popular music, and reading popular books and articles. Theme parks and museums are also considered sources of edutainment. While consuming media or frequenting places of this sort, these participants inadvertently learn something of substance about the social and physical world in which they live. They are, in a word, entertained and educated in the same breath.

Third, casual leisure affords regeneration, or re-creation, possibly even more so than its counterpart, serious leisure, since the latter can sometimes be intense. Of course, many a leisure studies specialist has observed that leisure in general affords relaxation or entertainment, if not both, and that these constitute two of its principal benefits. What is new, then, in the observation just made is that it distinguishes between casual and serious leisure, and more importantly, that it emphasizes the enduring effects of relaxation and entertainment when they help enhance overall equanimity, most notably in the interstices between periods of intense activity.

A fourth benefit that may flow from participation in casual leisure originates in the development and maintenance of interpersonal relationships. One of its types, the sociable conversation, is particularly fecund in this regard, but other types, when shared, as sometimes happens during sensory stimulation and passive and active entertainment, can also have the same effect. The interpersonal relationships in question are many and varied, and encompass those that form between friends, spouses, and members of families. Such relationships, Hutchinson and Kleiber (2005) found in a set of studies of some of the benefits of casual leisure, can foster personal psychological growth by promoting new shared interests and, in the course of this process, new positive appraisals of self.

Well-being is still another benefit that can flow from engaging in casual leisure. Speaking only for the realm of leisure, perhaps the greatest sense of well-being is achieved when a person develops an *OLL*. Such a lifestyle is "the deeply satisfying pursuit during free time of one or more substantial, absorbing forms of serious leisure, complemented by a judicious amount of casual leisure" (Stebbins 2007a). People find OLLs by partaking of leisure activities that individually and in combination realize human potential and enhance quality of life and well-being. Project-based leisure can also enhance a person's leisure lifestyle. The study of kayakers, snowboarders, and mountain and ice climbers (Stebbins 2005c) revealed that the vast majority of the three samples used various forms of casual leisure to optimally round out their use of free time. For them their serious leisure was a central life interest, but their casual leisure contributed to overall well-being by allowing for relaxation, regeneration, sociability, entertainment, and other activities less intense than their serious leisure.

Still well-being experienced during free time is more than this, as Hutchinson and Kleiber (2005) observed, since this kind of leisure can contribute to self-protection, as by buffering stress and sustaining coping efforts. Casual leisure can also preserve or restore a sense of self. This was sometimes achieved in their samples, when subjects said they rediscovered in casual leisure fundamental personal or familial values or a view of themselves as caring people.

Project-Based Leisure

Project-based leisure (Stebbins 2005b) is the third form of leisure activity and the most recent one added to the Perspective. It is a short-term, reasonably complicated, one-off or occasional, though infrequent, creative undertaking carried out in free time, or time free of disagreeable obligation. Such leisure requires considerable planning, effort, and sometimes skill or knowledge, but is for all that neither serious leisure nor intended to develop into such. The adjective "occasional" describes widely spaced undertakings for such regular occasions as religious festivals, someone's birthday, or a national holiday. Volunteering for a sports event may be seen as an occasional project. The adjective "creative" stresses that the undertaking results in something new or different, by showing imagination and perhaps routine skill or knowledge. Though most projects would appear to be continuously pursued until completed, it is conceivable that some might be interrupted for several weeks, months, even years (e.g., a stone wall in the back garden that gets finished only after its builder recovers from an operation on his strained back). Only a rudimentary social world springs up around the project, it does, in its own particular way, bring together friends, neighbors, or relatives (e.g., through a genealogical project or Christmas celebrations), or draw the individual participant into an organizational milieu (e.g., through volunteering for a sports event or major convention).

Moreover, it appears that, in some instances, project-based leisure springs from a sense of obligation to undertake it. If so, it is nonetheless, as leisure, uncoerced activity, in the sense that the obligation is in fact "agreeable"—the project creator in executing the project anticipates finding fulfillment, obligated to do so or not. And worth exploring in future research, given that some obligations can be pleasant and attractive, is the nature and extent of leisure-like projects carried out within the context of paid employment. Furthermore, this discussion jibes with the additional criterion that the project, to qualify as project-based leisure, must be *seen by the project creator* as fundamentally uncoerced, fulfilling activity. Finally, note that project-based leisure cannot, by definition, refer to projects executed as part of a person's serious leisure, such as mounting a star night as an amateur astronomer or a model train display as a collector.

Though not serious leisure, project-based leisure is enough like it to justify using the SLP to develop a parallel framework for exploring this neglected class of activities. A main difference is that project-based leisure fails to generate a sense of career. Otherwise, however, there is here need to persevere, some skill or knowledge may be required and, invariably, effort is called for. Also present are recognizable benefits, a special identity, and often a social world of sorts, though it appears, one usually less complicated than those surrounding many serious leisure activities. And perhaps it happens at times that, even if not intended at the moment as participation in a type of serious leisure, the skilled, artistic, or intellectual aspects of the project prove so attractive that the participant decides, after the fact, to make a leisure career of their pursuit as a hobby or an amateur activity.

Project-based leisure is also capable of generating many of the rewards experienced in serious leisure. And, as in serious leisure so in project-based leisure: these rewards constitute part of the motivational basis for pursuing such highly fulfilling activity. Furthermore, motivation to undertake a leisure project may have an organizational base, much as many other forms of leisure do (Stebbins 2002). My observations suggest that small groups, grassroots associations (volunteer groups with few or no paid staff), and volunteer organizations (paid-staff groups using volunteer help) are the most common types of organizations in which people undertake project-based leisure.

Motivationally speaking, project-based leisure may be attractive in substantial part because it does not demand long-term commitment, as serious leisure does. Even occasional projects carry with them the sense that the undertaking in question has a definite end and may even be terminated prematurely. Thus, project-based leisure is no central life interest (Dubin 1992). Rather it is viewed by participants as fulfilling (as distinguished from enjoyable or hedonic) activity that can be experienced comparatively quickly, though certainly not as quickly as casual leisure.

Project-based leisure fits into leisure lifestyle in its own peculiar way as interstitial activity, like some casual leisure but not like most serious leisure. It can therefore help shape a person's OLL. For instance, it can usually be pursued at times convenient for the participant. It follows that project-based leisure is nicely suited to people who, out of proclivity or extensive nonleisure obligations or both, reject serious leisure and, yet, who also have no appetite for a steady diet of casual leisure. Among the candidates for project-based leisure are people with heavy workloads; homemakers, mothers, and fathers with extensive domestic responsibilities; unemployed individuals who, though looking for work, still have time at the moment for (I suspect, mostly one-shot) projects; and avid serious leisure enthusiasts who want a temporary change in their leisure lifestyle. Retired people, who often do have time for plenty of free time, may find project-based leisure attractive as a way to add variety to their lifestyle. Beyond these special categories of participant, project-based leisure offers a form of substantial leisure to all adults, adolescents, and even children looking for something interesting and exciting to do in free time that is neither casual nor serious leisure.

Although, at most, only a rudimentary social world springs up around a project, it can in its own particular way bring together friends, neighbors, or relatives (e.g., through a genealogical project), or draw the individual participant into an organizational milieu (e.g., through volunteering for a sports event). This further suggests that project-based leisure often has, in at least two ways, potential for building community. One, it can bring into contact people who otherwise have no reason to meet, or at least meet frequently. Two, by way of event volunteering and other collective altruistic activity, it can contribute to carrying off community events and projects. Project-based leisure is not, however, civil labor, which must be classified as exclusively serious leisure (Rojek 2002).

Types of Project-Based Leisure

It was noted in the definition just presented that project-based leisure is not all the same. Whereas systematic exploration may reveal others, two types are evident at this time: one-shot projects and occasional projects. These are presented next using the classificatory framework for amateur, hobbyist, and volunteer activities developed earlier in this chapter.

One-Shot Projects

In all these projects people generally use the talents and knowledge they have at hand, even though for some projects they may seek certain instructions beforehand, including reading a book or taking a short course. And some projects resembling hobbyist activity participation may require a modicum of preliminary conditioning. Always, the goal is to undertake successfully the one-off project and nothing more, and sometimes a small amount of background preparation is necessary for this. It is possible that a survey would show that most project-based leisure is hobbyist in character and the next most common, a kind of voluntee ring. First, the following hobbyist-like projects have so far been identified:

- Making and tinkering:
  - Interlacing, interlocking, and knot-making from kits
  - Other kit assembly projects (e.g., stereo tuner, craft store projects)
  - Do-it-yourself projects done primarily for fulfillment, some of which may even be undertaken with minimal skill and knowledge (e.g., build a rock wall or a fence, finish a room in the basement, plant a special garden). This could turn into an irregular series of such projects, spread over many years, possibly even transforming the participant into a hobbyist.
- Liberal arts:
  - Genealogy (not as ongoing hobby)
  - Tourism: special trip, not as part of an extensive personal tour program, to visit different parts of a region, a continent, or much of the world
- Activity participation: long back-packing trip, canoe trip; one-off mountain ascent (e.g., Fuji, Rainier, Kilimanjaro)

One-off volunteering projects are also common, though possibly somewhat less so than hobbyist-like projects. And less common than either are the amateur-like projects, which seem to concentrate in the sphere of theater.

- Volunteering
  - Volunteer at a convention or conference, whether local, national, or international in scope.
  - Volunteer at a sporting competition, whether local, national, or international in scope.
  - Volunteer at an arts festival or special exhibition mounted in a museum.
  - Volunteer to help restore human life or wildlife after a natural or human-made disaster caused by, for instance, a hurricane, earthquake, oil spill, or industrial accident.
- Arts projects (this new category replaces Entertainment Theater, see Stebbins [2011a]):
  - Entertainment theater: produce a skit or one-off community pageant; prepare a home film, video, or set of photos.
  - Public speaking: prepare a talk for a reunion, an after-dinner speech, an oral position statement on an issue to be discussed at a community meeting.
  - Memoirs: therapeutic audio, visual, and written productions by the elderly; life histories and autobiographies (all ages); accounts of personal events (all ages) (Stebbins 2011a).

Occasional Projects

The occasional projects seem more likely to originate in or be motivated by agreeable obligation than their one-off cousins. Examples of occasional projects include the sum of the culinary, decorative, or other creative activities undertaken, for example, at home or at work for a religious occasion or someone's birthday. Likewise, national holidays and similar celebrations sometimes inspire individuals to mount occasional projects consisting of an ensemble of inventive elements.

Unlike one-off projects, occasional projects have the potential to become routinized, which happens when new creative possibilities no longer come to mind as the participant arrives at a fulfilling formula wanting no further modification. North Americans who decorate their homes the same way each Christmas season exemplify this situation. Indeed, it can happen that, over the years, such projects may lose their appeal, but not their necessity, thereby becoming disagreeable obligations, which their authors no longer define as leisure.

And, lest it be overlooked, note that one-off projects also hold the possibility of becoming unpleasant. Thus, the hobbyist genealogist gets overwhelmed with the details of family history and the challenge of verifying dates. The thought of putting in time and effort doing something once considered leisure but which she now dislikes makes no sense. Likewise, volunteering for a project may turn sour, creating in the volunteer a sense of being faced with a disagreeable obligation, which however, must still be honored. This is leisure no more.

Deviant Leisure

Viewed from the SLP, deviant leisure may occur in either the casual or the serious form (we have so far been unable to identify any project-based deviant leisure). Casual leisure deviance is probably the more common and widespread of the two. A review of some of the literature in this area is available (Stebbins 2007a, 65–67).

Casual or serious, deviant leisure mostly fits the description of "tolerable deviance" (exceptions are discussed below). Although its contravention of certain moral norms of a society is held by most of its members to be mildly threatening in most social situations, this form of deviance nevertheless fails to generate any significant or effective communal attempts to control it (Stebbins 1996b, 3–4). Tolerable deviance undertaken for pleasure—as casual leisure—encompasses a range of deviant sexual activities including cross-dressing, homosexuality, watching sex (e.g., striptease, pornographic films), and swinging and group sex. Heavy drinking and gambling, but not their more seriously regarded cousins alcoholism and compulsive gambling, are also tolerably deviant forms of casual leisure, as are the use of cannabis and the illicit, pleasurable, use of certain prescription drugs. Social nudism has also been analyzed within the tolerable deviance perspective (all these forms are examined in greater detail with accent on their leisure qualities in Stebbins [1996b, chaps. 3–7, 9]).

In the final analysis, deviant casual leisure roots in sensory stimulation and, in particular, the creature pleasures it produces. The majority of people in society tolerate most of these pleasures even if they would never think, or at least not dare, to enjoy themselves in these ways. In addition, they actively scorn a somewhat smaller number of intolerable forms of deviant casual leisure, demanding decisive police control of, for example, incest, vandalism, sexual assault, and what Jack Katz (1988, chap. 2) calls the "sneaky thrills" (certain incidents of theft, burglary, shoplifting, and joyriding). Sneaky thrills, however, are motivated not by the desire for creature pleasure, but rather by the desire for a special kind of excitement, namely, going against the grain of established social life.

Beyond the broad domains of tolerable and intolerable deviant casual leisure lies that of the deviant serious pursuits, composed primarily of aberrant religion, politics, and science engaged in as appealing work or leisure. Deviant religion is manifested in the sects and cults of the typical modern society, while deviant politics is constituted of the radical fringes of its ideological left and right. Deviant science centers on the occult which, according to Marcello Truzzi (1972), consists of five types: divination, witchcraft-Satanism, extrasensory perception, Eastern religious thought, and various residual occult phenomena revolving around UFOs, water witching, lake monsters, and the like (for further details, see Stebbins [1996b, chap. 10]). Thus the deviant serious pursuits are, in the main, pursued as liberal arts hobbies or as activity participation, or in fields like witchcraft and divination, as both.

In whichever form of deviant serious pursuit a person participates, he or she will find it necessary to make a significant effort to acquire its special belief system as well as to defend it against attack from mainstream science, religion, or politics. Moreover, here, the person will discover two additional rewards of considerable import: a special personal identity grounded, in part, in the unique genre of self-enrichment that invariably comes with inhabiting any marginal social world.

Youth Deviance

Leisure studies research, such as that of Iso-Ahola and Crowley (1991), shows that boredom in free time is an antecedent of deviant leisure, as when bored youth (the group most commonly examined) seek stimulation in drugs and alcohol or criminal thrills like gang fighting, illegal gambling, and joy riding in stolen cars. The authors were primarily concerned with substance abusers, citing research indicating that these deviants are more likely than nonabusers to seek thrilling and adventurous pursuits, while showing little taste for repetitious and constant experiences. In other words, such youth were looking for leisure that could give them optimal arousal, that was at the same time a regular activity—not sporadic like bungee jumping or roller coaster riding—but that did not, however, require long periods of monotonous preparation. Such preparation is necessary to become, for instance, a good football player or skateboarder.

To the extent that wayward youth have little or no taste for repetitious and constant experiences, then what kind of leisure will alleviate their boredom? Some forms of casual leisure, if accessible for them, can accomplish this, but do so only momentarily. Such leisure is by definition fleeting. As for serious leisure, though all activities do require significant levels of perseverance, not all require repetitious preparation of the kind needed, say, to learn a musical instrument or train for a sport. For example, none of the volunteer activities and liberal arts hobbies calls for such preparation. The same can be said for amateur science, hobbyist collecting, various games, and many activity participation fields. Spelunking, orienteering, and some kinds of sports volunteering exemplify nonrepetitive serious leisure that is both exciting and, with the first two, reasonably adventurous.

Yet, the problem here is, rather, more one of lack of known and accessible activities that amount to true leisure, than one of being forced into inactivity or to do something boring. Being coerced suggests to the coerced person that no palatable escape from his condition exists. Thus, he must work, since money for necessities will come from nowhere else, or he must give the mugger his money or risk getting shot or beaten. With boring activities, however, palatable alternatives do exist, some of which are deviant, as we have just seen, some of which are not.

Those that are not deviant must nevertheless be brought to light, which is a central goal of leisure education. But what would leisure educators (including leisure counselors and leisure volunteers) teach to chronically bored youth? In general, they should focus not on so much casual leisure but on serious and project-based leisure (this approach is discussed in Stebbins [2010b]). This is not the last word on the matter.

Conclusion

The SLP is both individual and contextual in scope. Looking closely at the individual component, it is possible to discern another first principle, namely, that leisure is what a person does in free time. People, when they think of about free time, also think about what they do during it and what that means to them. If asked they can give a list of the general activities pursued here. They can also evaluate these activities as, say, intensely interesting (a serious leisure passion), as moderately interesting (e.g., a leisure project), or as not very interesting (a common complaint about some television programming). Furthermore, they can speak about their past leisure activities and the ones they would like to take up in the future.

This seventh principle is primarily descriptive—what one does—whereas the sixth principle on leisure's role in achieving work/life balance, introduced in the preceding chapter, is utilitarian. Here, leisure is conceived of as useful (immensely so) in finding an agreeable equilibrium for all of life's everyday activities. The eighth principle—the unique image by which leisure is known in the larger world—is examined in the next chapter. This principle is cultural, in that it expresses the collective, or communal, view of leisure.

5

Leisure's Image in the Twenty-First Century

Leisure in modern society does not exist in vacuum. In harmony with this observation the present chapter explores an eighth principle of leisure, or the unique image by which it is known in the larger world. To be precise, we should say the larger Western world, for we lack data on such an image in countries outside it. Leisure has a unique public image in the West, an image rooted in the seven principles forged in the preceding chapters. And this is a good point in this book to present a full list of the first principles, the properties of leisure that distinguish it from all other phenomenon, gained in part by widening the conceptual scope of leisure to include devotee work. They are

1. leisure is uncoerced (general) activity;
2. leisure is core activity that participants want to do;
3. leisure is pursued in free time, defined as time away from disagreeable obligation;
4. leisure is a social institution;
5. leisure has its own geographic space (the pure type);
6. leisure is the fulcrum for work/life balance;
7. leisure is what a person does in free time;
8. leisure is known in the larger world by a unique image.

These eight principles and the theoretical and empirical support for them presented throughout this book constitute a set of propositions showing how the idea of leisure could become the vision that supplants the idea of progress, which now seems to be stalled. It is difficult to speak convincingly these days about progress in general, but meanwhile leisure is gaining ground. True, leisure's advance has sometimes been of the two-steps-forward-one-step-backward variety (see, for example, the next section on leisure's negative image), but there is plenty of reason to believe that, overall, leisure is making noticeable headway as a major vehicle for human and communal development.

The preceding chapters offer a good deal of evidence for this claim. In this sense the spread of leisure is progress, but it is, however, only one kind of progress. Ironically, as mentioned in the Introduction, the early thinkers trumpeting progress did not even have leisure in their musical score.

That the SLP has now been extended into seventeen different areas of theory and practice beyond the field of leisure studies is presented here as evidence that the idea of leisure has progressed, that leisure is progressive. Put otherwise leisure's public image is complex, and I will not attempt in this chapter to examine its every detail. Rather to make the point, to show the grand lines of this image, I will first consider its negative and then its positive aspects. A fuller statement must await some methodological developments. For we have yet to create a survey instrument by which we can measure this image, which preliminary observations suggest, varies greatly across the population of every Western nation.

Leisure's Negative Image

"For Satan finds some mischief still for idle hands to do," proclaimed Issac Watts some 300 years ago. Today negative views of leisure tend not to be of this genre (though some observations on boredom come close, e.g., Brissett and Snow [1993]), but rather take a different tact. Thus, we saw in Chapter 2 that the work ethic of modern times stresses that a person should work, work hard, and avoid leisure as much as possible. Work is good, while leisure is not (although a little of it after a good day's work is acceptable). Indeed the history of leisure presented in that chapter shows the different image problems leisure has had to face with passage of time.

Alternatively leisure is sometimes seen today as frivolous, as simply having a good time, or in the language of leisure studies, as casual leisure and the quest for hedonism. The image of frivolity fades off into that of leisure as a waste of time, because frivolousness is believed by some people to lead to nothing substantial even while several benefits of casual leisure have been identified (Hutchinson and Kleiber 2005; Kleiber 2000; Stebbins, 2001c). A related image is that leisure is unimportant, in the sense that there is little need to plan for it, that what we do in free time can be determined on the spot.

Finally, as pointed out in the preceding chapter, some leisure is deviant. In line with the theme of the present chapter, such activity, to the extent the larger society sees it in unfavorable terms while defining it as leisure, also has a public image as such. Note, however, that the deviants themselves may not embrace this image of their questionable activities. Note, too, that negativeness of the image is stronger in cases of intolerable deviance than in those held to be tolerable. Surely we would, for example, view with greater intolerance serial murder as leisure (Gunn and Cassie 2006) than gamers' social construction of violent video game play as leisure (Delamere and Shaw 2006).

The study of deviant leisure is for the most part a decade and a half old (see Cantwell 2003; Rojek 1997, 392–93; 2000, chap. 4; Stebbins 1996b, 1997; special issue of *Leisure/Loisir*, v. 30, no. 1, 2006), and readers interested in it are encouraged to turn to these sources. What is important to observe with respect to the matter of leisure's public image is that deviant leisure may assume either the casual or the serious form (we have so far been unable to identify any project-based deviant leisure). Casual leisure is probably the more common and widespread of the two, though not necessarily the more tolerable. These expressions of deviant leisure were discussed in Chapter 4.

Leisure's Positive Image

Probably most people see leisure in both a negative and a positive light. Whatever they think about leisure in general as, frivolous, insubstantial, unimportant, or deviant, or a combination of these evaluations, they also see leisure in at least two positive ways. One, they commonly see it as fun, as manifested in participants smiling, laughing, and being at ease with what they are doing. Hence, the concentration of the serious leisure athlete or performing artist, for example, is incongruous for them, possibly not even really leisure. Two, they look fondly on their own leisure as something positive. They want to pursue their personal leisure, for here they find satisfaction or fulfillment, if not both. In fact this book has been a journey into the world of positive leisure for its participants, showing in detail what they gain from their free-time involvements as well as how they see in favorable terms these benefits and rewards.

We have been speaking here of the way the general public tends to regard leisure as positive activity. But there is another angle from which to view leisure as positive. That angle is the one of leisure application. Professionals in a fair range of applied sciences have drawn on leisure theory and research to help inform effective practice. I am not referring here to application of such theory and research to practical problems commonly considered the province of leisure studies, for example, those centered on parks, forests, leisure services, and leisure policy. Rather I have in mind a miscellany of applied disciplines whose origins lie outside leisure studies but who have found significant nourishment in the second.

Now it has been argued that practitioners in these applied disciplines are seriously unaware of what the field of leisure studies has learned about leisure. Thus, Samdahl and Kelly (1999) have observed that far too often we fail to familiarize inform the larger world with about theory and research in leisure, be that world other academic and applied disciplines or the general public. After a review of the two main leisure studies journals in the United States, the two authors also concluded that leisure studies specialists seldom cite articles on leisure published outside the leisure studies literature. Meanwhile, writers in this external literature seldom cite articles in the two journals. Additionally, Susan Shaw (2000) holds that when we do try to talk to people outside leisure studies, no one listens. Others have held that there is a paucity of theory in leisure studies (e.g., Searle 2000); argue that its research is methodologically deficient (e.g., Witt 2000, 188); or that the typical research problems are banal (Samdahl 2000, 125) or irrelevant (Kelly 2000). These are said to be additional reasons for the failure of leisure studies to make an impact beyond its disciplinary borders.

What we have here is intellectual apartheid, real and regrettable. I remain unconvinced, however, by the arguments about deficient or uninteresting theory, methodology, and research problems. One, there is plenty of theory in leisure studies (see Rojek 2005). Two, these charges can and should also be leveled at a number of other social sciences. Many a modern social science boasts numerous small theories constructed to explain a little corner of the larger discipline. Very few of these sciences have all-encompassing theories that pull together most or all of their research and small-theoretic developments (perhaps, economics is the main exception).

If these other sciences are weak for these same reasons, they too should be ignored by outsiders. Yet, anthropology, archaeology, and psychology, for example, seem to enjoy considerable credibility in the outside world, while festering internal theoretical and methodological differences stir noticeable levels of acrimony and confusion. Furthermore, what proof do we have that researchers, practitioners, and the general public even know about these internal criticisms in leisure studies (or in the other social sciences)? In short, we may question whether these theoretical and methodological "weaknesses" are giving leisure studies a rough ride both now and in the future.

In fact leisure does have a positive image in quite number of disciplines, most of them primarily applied. These disciplines have learned about the SLP, and have adopted aspects of it relevant to their interests. Sometimes word about the SLP has come from within, in that one or more insiders have imported certain parts of the Perspective. On other occasions a leisure studies specialist has exported observations from the SLP to a particular applied discipline.

The remainder of this chapter is devoted to presenting seven examples of this kind of cross-fertilization. They are drawn from the following list of seventeen fields where this process is now underway in some degree:

- Tourism
- Ethnicity
- Quality of Life/Well-Being
- Leisure Education
- Gender
- Retirement/Unemployment
- Disabilities/Therapeutic Recreation
- Library and Information Science (LIS)
- Entertainment and Popular Culture
- Arts Administration (e.g., museums, arts festivals)
- Consumption
- Contemplation
- Adult Education/Lifelong Learning
- Nonprofit Sector
- Youth/Delinquency
- Social Entrepreneurship
- Event Studies

Eight of these will be more closely examined below: LIS, disabilities/therapeutic recreation, adult education and lifelong learning, consumption, event analysis, arts administration, youth and juvenile delinquency, and youth and world peace. Each field will be described and its relationship to the SLP set out, both done in the interest of showing how the image of leisure has pervaded the field in question. All seventeen could be portrayed in this manner, but treating seven of them this way should make the point about this facet of leisure's image in the twenty-first century.

Library and Information Science

Bates (1999, 1044) defines the interdisciplinary field of library science, or LIS, as "the study of the gathering, organizing, storing, retrieving, and dissemination of information." She points out that this field cuts across conventional academic disciplines, as its researchers engage in such "processes" as information seeking, teaching, and learning. This is done along lines of various "domains," or universes of recorded information, that are developed and retained for later access. LIS is both a pure science and a practical one, with the latter concentrated on developing services and products for specialties like journalism and library science. Historically, library science and information science were separate disciplines, and the first continues within the framework of LIS to study the goals and justifications of the occupational craft of librarianship.

Jenna Hartel has pioneered the extension of serious leisure into LIS. Hartel (2003) points out that, historically, LIS has leaned heavily toward studying scholarly and professional informational domains, while largely ignoring those related to leisure (negative image of leisure as unimportant). In an attempt to help redress this imbalance, she introduces the study of information in hobbies. Serious leisure is examined for its library and informational forces and properties as these relate to a particular core leisure activity and the organizational milieu in which it is pursued. It is known that the patterns of storage, retrieval, and dissemination vary considerably from one core activity to another. Hartel has been currently conducting research that explores these patterns in the hobby of cooking. Other researchers are examining, for example, information use and dissemination among back packers and coin collectors (see *Library Trends*, v. 57, no. 4, 2009).

Disabilities/Therapeutic Recreation

Patterson (2001) challenges the idea that leisure experiences are unimportant for people with disabilities. He points out that serious leisure activities are complex and profound, and that for all people, including the disabled, they can become a source of self-respect and self-esteem. This condition leads, in turn, to greater acceptance and social inclusion in the wider community.

Patterson has continued to extend serious leisure into the field of disabilities studies and practice. For instance, he has recommended that community-based agencies serving people with disabilities implement leisure counseling and educational services as well as hire trained leisure counselors to support their clients (Patterson 2000). Given the subsequent addition of project-based leisure to the Perspective, I now add that form of leisure to this exhortation. In a later paper Patterson (2001) argues that we should center our leisure education programs for the intellectually disabled on serious leisure activities. Such activities can engender self-respect, self-esteem, and lead to greater acceptance and social inclusion in the larger community. Aitchison (2003, 956) adds for people with disabilities in general that pursuing serious leisure

The following exemplifies the use and dissemination of information in the hobby of cooking:

Step	Information practices	Information resources
Exploring	Imagining, browsing, reading, talking	Recipes, cookbooks, serials, reference sources, web pages, culinary databases, homemade compilations, people
Planning	Seeking, searching, comparing, producing	Recipes, cookbooks, serials, reference sources, web pages, culinary databases, homemade compilations, lists, timelines/ schedules
Provisioning	Use (reuse)	Recipes, promotional and sales materials, lists
Prepping	Use (reuse)	Recipes, cookbooks, serials, reference sources, timelines/ schedules
Assembling	Use (reuse)	Recipes, cookbooks, serials, reference sources, timelines/ schedules
Cooking	Use (reuse)	Recipes, cookbooks, serials, reference sources, timelines/ schedules
Serving	Use (reuse)	Recipes, cookbooks, serials, reference sources, timelines/ schedules
Eating	Nonuse, talking	[The senses]
Evaluating	Use (reuse), records, talking	Recipes, culinary records, people

Source: Taken from Hartel (2003).

may enhance physical health and fitness as well as reduce risk of illness. For the reason just given, we can also add project-based leisure to this recommendation for programs in leisure education.

Neuro-Rehabilitation

Turning to the field of neuro-rehabilitation, leisure has been, for some time, among the tools used in rehabilitating people afflicted with neuro-disabilities. Rehabilitation programs for such people include the goals of helping them reenter the larger community, develop their leisure interests, and even acquire a certain level of leisure education. These programs further incorporate some occupational therapy aimed at increasing the client's capacity to physically meet, within limits of the disability, not only self-maintenance needs like eating, toileting, grooming, and dressing, but also routine work and leisure needs peculiar to the activities this person engages in there. Thanks to such programs people with neuro-disabilities are no longer consigned to the margin, forced to watch from the sidelines life being played out by the nondisabled. Now after participating in one of these programs a fuller, more rewarding lifestyle on society's main playing field is possible.

Nevertheless, from the standpoint of leisure, there is still room for improvement. And this notwithstanding the progress made in this area. To this end, Stebbins (2008a) explored the role of the SLP in neuro-rehabilitation. Leisure as a tool for rehabilitating people with neuro-disabilities was, by the time of his article, well established. Yet, despite significant progress in this area, problems remain in the way leisure was being used for this purpose. One, as yet, unresolved problem is how to determine which leisure activity or activities will be attractive to people with particular disabilities. Another is how to counteract the persistent, dominant public view that real personal worth is measured according to the work people do rather than the leisure they pursue (cf. leisure's negative image). The third is to inform practitioners, many of whom are unaware of recent advances in leisure theory, about these advances, which can help them solve the first problem and adapt to the second. The main body of the Stebbins presents such a theory, namely, the SLP. A review of the research on neuro-rehabilitation follows. Some implications of the Perspective for neuro-rehabilitation are then presented, including ways practitioners can introduce clients to certain types of leisure, encourage them to pursue the types chosen, and help them develop an OLL.

How can both therapists and people with neuro-disabilities find their way around the typological map presented as Figure 4.1 in the preceding chapter? A suggested point of departure is, given the disability in question, to determine which types of serious leisure and activities within those types are feasible for a particular client. Next, for these feasible, serious leisure areas of the map, determine which types and activities match that person's tastes, natural talents, and personal interests. That is try to develop a list of, say, a half-dozen, serious leisure activities that offer as strong as possible an opportunity for finding self-fulfillment and in which actual participation is appealing. Finally, choose one of these, or more if the client has time and energy for learning how to do them. This leads to the goal of building an OLL for people with disabilities, defined earlier as pursuing one or more deeply fulfilling serious leisure activities during free time, complemented by a judicious amount of casual or project-based leisure or both.

Adult Education/Lifelong Learning

Since the link between adult education and leisure has been examined elsewhere in detail (Stebbins 2001a, 94–102), we need here only describe, in broad terms, this link. This will set the stage for a longer discussion on lifelong learning and the SLP. As a guide for this chapter, we will use the definition of adult education prepared by UNESCO:

> Adult education is the entire body of organized educational processes, whatever the content, level and method, whether formal or otherwise, whether they prolong or replace initial education in schools, colleges and universities as well as apprenticeship, whereby persons regarded as adult by the society to which they belong develop their abilities, enrich their knowledge, improve their technical or professional qualifications or turn them in a new direction and bring about changes in their attitudes or behavior in the twofold perspective of full personal development and participation in balanced and independent social, economic and cultural development. (UNESCO 1976, 2)

Learning—adult learning in particular—is the object of these educational processes. "Continuing education" often refers to the same processes, although the idea usually connotes furthering a person's education beyond initial education undertaken as preparation for a work role (Jarvis 1995, 29).

Roberson (2005, 205) notes the crucial differences between adult education and self-directed learning and then links the second to serious leisure. Drawing on an earlier conceptualization by Lambdin (1997), he says that "self-directed learning is intentional and self-planned learning where the individual is clearly in control of this process." Such learning may be formal (here it would be synonymous with adult education), but most often, it is informal. An important condition is that the learner controls the start, direction, and termination of the learning experience. Both adult education and self-directed learning are types of "lifelong learning." The latter is a broader idea than the first two, summarized by Selman and colleagues (1998, 21) as learning done throughout a person's lifetime, "from the cradle to the grave."

In general, and in harmony with the emphasis in leisure education, adult education centers, for the most part, on serious rather than casual leisure. Such education can also be pursued, however, as a leisure project. For instance, amateurs in many arts and scientific fields avail themselves of adult education courses, and in the arts, even whole programs, that further their learning of a serious leisure activity. The same can be said for most of the individual amateur sports (e.g., golf, tennis, racquetball). Still, if we examine all the adult educational programs available in the typical North American city, it becomes clear that they ignore some amateur activities (e.g., handball, rodeo, weight lifting as well as auto and motorcycle racing and virtually all the entertainment arts, Stebbins [2001a, 97]).

Adult education is also, with the exception of collecting, a main avenue for learning hobbies. A great range of making and tinkering activities fill the multitude of North American adult education catalogs, including baking, decorating, do-it-yourself, raising and breeding, and various crafts (for a discussion of the many different hobbies, see Stebbins [1998, chap. 3]). The same is true for activity participation, which includes such diverse enthusiasms as scuba diving, cross-country skiing, mushroom gathering, and ballroom dancing as well as a few of the hobbyist activities and sports and games (e.g., bridge, orienteering, and the martial arts). On the other hand the liberal arts hobbies are most often acquired purely through self-direction, chiefly by reading, as noted earlier. But here, too, we find exceptions, as in the general interest courses offered on certain arts, cultures, philosophies, and histories. Indeed, language instruction is one of the pillars of adult education.

Adult education courses related to volunteerism center mostly in such areas as fund raising, accounting and book-keeping, and management and recruitment of volunteers. To the extent that serious leisure volunteers are involved in these areas, they are likely to be interested in courses bearing on them. Still many career volunteers devote themselves to other tasks, which they learn outside the framework of adult education. That is, the group (club, society, association, organization) in which they serve provides the basic instruction they need to learn further while on the job.

Consonant with Houle's (1961) distinction between learning-oriented and goal-oriented motives for pursuing adult education is the fact that the liberal arts hobbies are the only form of serious leisure where learning is an end in itself. By contrast, amateurs, volunteers, and other hobbyists learn as a means to particular leisure ends, such as producing art, playing sport, collecting objects, or helping others. Sometimes both types of participant enroll in the same course, a pattern that may be especially common in science. Thus, some students in an adult education astronomy course may be liberal arts hobbyists, while others are there to learn about the heavens as background for their research.

Jones and Symon (2001) have argued that lifelong learning is a kind of serious leisure (more precisely a liberal arts hobby), and that governmental policy and practice should reflect this fact. The usual rewards that flow from all serious leisure are also found in lifelong learning. Therefore such learning is not to be dismissed as casual leisure, as hedonism, which governments are inclined to do given the stereotype that leisure is solely hedonic.

In general, and in harmony with the emphasis in leisure education, adult education centers, for the most part, on serious rather than casual leisure. Such education can also be pursued, however, as a leisure project. For instance amateurs in many arts and scientific fields avail themselves of adult education courses, and in the arts, even whole programs, that further their learning of a serious leisure activity. The same can be said for most of the individual amateur sports (e.g., golf, tennis, racquetball). Still, if we examine all the adult educational programs available in the typical North American city, it becomes clear that they ignore some amateur activities (e.g., handball, rodeo, weight lifting as well as auto and motorcycle racing and virtually all the entertainment arts, Stebbins [2001a, 97]).

Adult education is also, with the exception of collecting, a main avenue for learning hobbies. A great range of making and tinkering activities fill the multitude of North American adult education catalogs, including baking, decorating, do-it-yourself, raising and breeding, and various crafts (for a discussion of the many different hobbies, see Stebbins [1998 , chap. 3]). The same is true for activity participation, which includes such diverse enthusiasms as scuba diving, cross-country skiing, mushroom gathering, and ballroom dancing as well as a few of the hobbyist activities and sports and games (e.g., bridge, orienteering, and the martial arts). On the other hand, the liberal arts hobbies are most often acquired purely through self-direction, chiefly by reading, as noted earlier. But here, too, we find exceptions, as in the general interest courses offered on certain arts, cultures, philosophies, and histories. Indeed, language instruction is one of the pillars of adult education.

Consumption

Consumption, says Russell Belk (2007, 737), "consists of activities potentially leading to and actually following from the acquisition of a good or service by those engaging in such activities." This is *monetary acquisition*, defined as either buying or renting with money a good or service. Hence bartering, borrowing, stealing, begging, and other forms of nonmonetary acquisition are deliberately excluded from this definition. Moreover, consumption through monetary acquisition is intentional. So receiving gifts also falls beyond the purview of this chapter, since intention resides in the giver, not the receiver.

Consumption studies, which describes and explains consumers, their consumptive behavior, and the creation, distribution, and purchase of the goods and services they consume, is a decidedly interdisciplinary field. Yet, the field is not as interdisciplinary as it might be, and I have argued recently (Stebbins 2009b), should be. That is specialists in this domain have failed to systematically consider leisure in their explanations of consumers and their consumptive behavior. As with consumption leisure may be analyzed and understood through the lens of all the institutions just mentioned, even work (e.g., Stebbins 2004a, 2011b). Yet, leisure in these institutions is by no means always consumptive. In fact, leisure and consumption have a very complex relationship with each other. I argue in the following pages, after Ken Roberts (1999, 179) and Jackie Kiewa (2003, 80), that, in no way, can all of leisure be equated with consumption, even mass consumption.

In other words, leisure and consumption are not always an identity. But Daniel Cook, for example, fails to see it this way: "We don't live near or beside consumer society, but within it. Consequently we don't seek, experience, make or find leisure and recreation anywhere else"

(Cook 2006, 313). McDonald, Wearing, and Ponting (2007, 495) hold that leisure "has become an escape from the pressures of the competitive individualized labour market through the process of therapeutic consumption. The importance placed upon the acquisition and consumption of commodities has resulted in fetishism...over-consumption, luxury fever...." That is, it is common in scholarly circles to view leisure as little more than purchase of a good or service. Accordingly my overall goal in Stebbins (2009b) was to clarify and explain where consumption and taking leisure are separate processes, where they are similar if not the same, and in such overlap, what that looks like. This clarification and explanation was missing in the literatures on consumption and leisure.

To present a more accurate picture of the relationship of consumption and leisure, I framed consumer behavior in the SLP. I started by observing that a substantial amount of consumption today has little or nothing to do with leisure, exemplified in buying toothpaste, life insurance, accounting services, natural gas for home heating, transit tickets for getting to work, and so forth. Such consumption, call it *obligatory consumption*, shows in itself that we cannot regard leisure (uncoerced activity) and consumption as the same.

In *leisure-based consumption*—it is critical to distinguish whether the leisure component of a particular activity is directly and solely dependent on acquiring a good or service (e.g., buying a CD, concert ticket, or a session of massage) or whether purchase of something is but prerequisite to a set of conditions that, much more centrally, shapes the activity as a leisure experience. In other words, is consumption an initiator or facilitator of a leisure experience? In *initiatory, leisure-based consumption* someone buys, say, a ticket allowing entrance to a cinema, a CD enabling listening to recorded music, a new sporty car enabling pleasurable motoring, or a club membership allowing fine drinking and dining with valued members. In such consumption the purchaser proceeds more or less directly to use the purchased item. Here, leisure and consumption are inextricably intertwined—an identity—even while sense of the initial consumption may fade as the owner replays for the tenth time the CD or drives six months later the flashy new automobile.

Not so with *facilitative, leisure-based consumption*. Here, the acquired item only sets in motion a set of activities, which when completed, enable the purchaser to use the item in a satisfying or fulfilling leisure experience. This is hardly the alienating consumption about which the critics of mass society wrote. As an example note that amateur violinists, if they are to play at all, must first rent or purchase a violin—a consumptive act. Yet, their most profound leisure experience is competently and artistically playing music and, earlier, practicing to accomplish this, all of which costs nothing, though, obviously, it is certainly facilitated by using the acquired instrument (a consumer product). Moreover, this profound leisure experience might be further facilitated by buying music lessons and transit tickets (to travel to a teacher's studio).

In this last example one or more purchases or rentals are necessary to experience the cherished leisure. Still, leisure activities exist for which little or no facilitative consumption is needed to participate in them, where consumption and leisure are clearly separate spheres. This is *nonconsumptive leisure* (Stebbins 2009b, 118–26). Such pursuits abound in casual and serious leisure, with nonconsumptive projects being possible as well.

Event Studies

Don Getz (2008, 405) states that "events studies" appeared to have been coined as a term in 2000, where reference was made to the field in passing by him in a speech (as early as 1993 Getz had been writing about "event tourism"). Since 2000 the field has blossomed, owing in good part to the pioneering work done there by Getz himself. The field centers on planned events, of which there are eight types:

- CULTURAL CELEBRATIONS (festivals, carnivals, commemorations, religious events)
- POLITICAL AND STATE (summits, royal occasions, political events, VIP visits)
- ARTS AND ENTERTAINMENT (concerts, award ceremonies)
- BUSINES AND TRADE (meetings, conventions, consumer and trade shows, fairs, markets)
- EDUCATIONAL AND SCIENTIFIC (conferences, seminars, clinics)
- SPORT COMPETITION (amateur/professional, spectator/participant)
- RECREATIONAL (sport or games for fun)
- PRIVATE EVENTS (weddings, parties, socials)
  (*Source:* Getz 2008, 404.)

Planned events occur in particular spaces at particular times. Each is unique, because of the way people interact within the setting and relate to the management system and the event's program. Indeed, this uniqueness constitutes a substantial part of the appeal of events; interested participants must attend to get the full experience, which will never be possible to obtain once the event is terminated. Nowadays there are also "virtual events," which can be experienced by way of a variety of media.

Events studies "is the academic field devoted to creating knowledge and theory about planned events. The core phenomenon is the experience of planned events and meanings attached to them" (Getz 2007, 4). This area is highly interdisciplinary, drawing on among other fields that of leisure studies. In his 2007 book, which may well be the first and so far the only textbook on the subject, Getz devotes eleven pages (128–38) to the place of leisure studies in event analysis. He sees serious leisure as helping to explain how people become involved in planned events, owing to their commitment to participating in them possibly to the extent that they find a leisure career in pursuing such activity.

Arts Administration

Application of the SLP to arts administration dates to research by Noreen Orr (2003), in which she examined museum volunteering as serious leisure and to Margaret Graham (2004), who studied from the same angle volunteers working in heritage museums. Then, Stebbins (2005d) published an occasional paper, in which he applied the overall SLP to arts administration.

Stebbins observed that most people who attend arts events (e.g., concerts, festivals, performances, exhibitions) or patronize arts facilities (e.g., galleries, museums, libraries) are seeking a leisure experience. Thus of use to arts administrators, whose job is, in part, to market the arts they have been hired to manage, is knowledge about this experience, particularly knowledge about its nature and its distribution in the population of potential arts buffs and consumers. Stebbins examined how consumption of the arts is differently realized in three forms of leisure: serious, casual, and project-based.

Amateurs and hobbyists in a given art constitute a small, but important, part of the public the arts administrator is trying to reach. That is, most people who attend an arts event or patronize an arts facility—i.e., the public of the art in question—are not themselves serious participants in it. They are not, for example, amateur painters or musicians or hobbyist quilters or coin collectors. Still, for the administrator, these amateurs and hobbyists are special. They do know the art intimately. Through this knowledge and experience, they may have some useful ideas on how to present it. Furthermore, if they like what they see or hear, they are in a position, because of their deep involvement in the social world of the art, to spread the word about a particular concert, exposition, collection, and the like. They may also be counted on to argue publicly and politically for the importance of the art in question and financially for its continued community and governmental support. And they themselves may be, or may become, significant donors.

Liberal arts hobbyists, as part of the art public, occupy a unique place there: they are *buffs*. They must be distinguished from their casual leisure counterparts: the *fans*. Buffs have, consistent with their serious leisure classification, considerable knowledge of and experience with their specialized interest in the art being presented. Fans, by contrast, consume the art for the enjoyment and pleasure this can bring; it is at bottom a hedonic activity requiring little or no background skill, knowledge, or experience.

Arts volunteers, as such, are not members of the public of a particular art, but are, rather, unpaid helpers who assist in presenting the art to its public. Among the career, volunteer roles in the arts are those of guide (often in a museum), receptionist, and member of the board of directors of an arts facility. Moreover, serious leisure arts volunteers may also be amateurs or hobbyists in the same art and, in that capacity, also members of its public. Such people have thus a dual serious leisure involvement in their art.

A powerful motive underlying the pursuit of all serious leisure is the search for deep self-fulfillment. Self-fulfillment is either the act or the process of developing to the full one's capacity, more particularly, developing one's gifts and character. Pursuing a fulfilling activity leads to such fulfillment. Since arts administrators hold considerable responsibility for setting the core tasks and working conditions of their volunteers, they also affect the level of fulfillment the latter can receive in this role.

Although they constitute only a minority of the public of a given art, the serious leisure amateurs, hobbyists, and liberal arts buffs contribute disproportionately to its survival and development. For this reason they, along with major donors, are worthy of occasional special treatment given, if possible, at little or no charge. Examples include exclusive invitations to workshops, receptions, special openings, preevent seminars, and meet-the-artist gatherings.

Casual Leisure

Turning to casual leisure and arts administration, note that people seeking a casual leisure experience in the arts tend to approach them as relatively passive consumers. Still, as in serious leisure, volunteers serving in casual leisure roles are special. In that role they are hardly passive consumers, but rather active helpers. Here, vis-à-vis arts administration, they perform a variety of useful functions, ranging from taking and selling tickets, handing out programs, and giving directions to ushering, serving drinks (when paid bartenders are not used), and stuffing envelopes. If properly designed and managed these activities can be enjoyable, a responsibility that falls to the arts administrator.

The discussion to this point about serious and casual leisure and arts administration is summarized in Figure 5.1.

Project-Based Leisure

The project-based leisure of greatest interest to arts administrators is, by and large, the one-shot variety and involves volunteers. Organizers of arts festivals and certain expositions in museums have need

Figure 5.1 Serious and Casual Leisure in Arts Administration

SERIOUS LEISURE

```
            Public                          Volunteers
          /        \
  Amateurs        Hobbyists                 examples:
                   |                        - board member
                   |                        - guide
            Liberal Arts Buffs              - receptionist

    Reward:  deep fulfillment              deep fulfillment
```

CASUAL LEISURE

```
    Public-Consumers                       Volunteers

    - sensory stimulation                  examples:
    - passive entertainment                - take/sell tickets
    - active entertainment                 - hand out programs
    - relaxation                           - give directions
    - sociable conversation                - usher
    - play                                 - serve drinks
                                           - stuff envelops

    Reward: enjoyment                      enjoyment
```

for a number of one-time, project-based volunteers. Although, it was observed that this form of leisure is distinct from serious leisure, both forms offer the same list of motivating rewards. Furthermore, project-based leisure requires considerable planning and effort as well as, at times, skill or knowledge and for this reason, its participants expect a fulfilling experience. As with serious leisure, it is largely up to the arts administrator to ensure that this happens.

Some Administrative Challenges

Although having publics composed of seekers of both serious and casual leisure may be appreciated by the arts administrator for their diversity, however disproportionate the two groups, this diversity also generates a number of challenges. One challenge is finding the best balance of offerings and commentary about them, such that large segments of both groups are routinely attracted to the event or the facility. For instance, hobbyist collectors may want extensive written material on the collectibles displayed, whereas casual consumers usually seem happy simply to look at them without reading much of what is posted there.

Then there is the challenge, found in some arts, of achieving a balance of offerings representing both their fine art and popular-commercial sides. The commercial facet is more popular and consequently draws a significantly larger number of casual leisure consumers compared with the fine arts facet, which amateurs, hobbyists, and liberal arts buffs like, even while it lacks mass appeal. For instance, professional symphony orchestras in North America know very well that they can bring in considerably more income with a couple of concerts of Strauss waltzes or Broadway shows tunes than they can with the same number of concerts devoted exclusively to the works of, say, nineteenth-century classical composers. And, on the theatrical stage, Gilbert and Sullivan will sell to the general public much better than Ibsen or Brecht.

Leisure, these pages show, is for many reasons, an important consideration for arts administrators. Good administration in this sphere increases exposure of the art and enhances the financial status of the artists displayed. Administrators are therefore key players in the success of many arts occupations. Moreover, they have this effect, in significant part, because they understand the leisure interests of their serious and casual leisure patrons and volunteers and because they imaginatively apply this knowledge to organizing presentations of the arts in their charge.

Youth and Juvenile Delinquency

Caldwell and Smith (2007) suggest that, as an antidote delinquency, youth be informed of the SLP. They also urge that youth be encouraged to gain a stake in mainstream life by developing a commitment to one or more serious leisure activities. Still the prospect of adolescent serious leisure raises some thorny questions.

Even if they are seldom, or never, involved with professionals as adult amateurs may be and often are, some adolescents do nevertheless appear to pursue certain serious leisure activities with adult-like passion, commitment, and perseverance, and so on just as older participants do. Nevertheless, they may be marginalized for this by the prevailing youth culture, with its powerful accent on casual leisure. Thus we need to learn more about, for instance, the lifestyles and social worlds of teenagers active in all types of serious leisure and about how they manage their leisure as full-time students and participants in family and peer-group activities (see Spector 2007).

The problem for practitioners is how to counteract the present-day, widespread tendency for youth to devote much of their waking lives to activities that lead to little or no profound personal development. The goal among a large majority of them, after the disagreeable obligations of life are either met or ignored (often those associated with school or work), is to have "fun." The recent crazes in the use of iPads, MP3 players, cell phones, video gaming facilities, and the like spring from a long-standing interest in hedonic activities that, in the past, was evident in, partying, watching television, going to the cinema, hanging out (in bars, restaurants, street corners), lying on beaches, to mention but a few. Their image of leisure excludes the serious and project-based forms.

Nonetheless, for society, the payoff of knowledge about adolescent involvement in serious leisure could be considerable. For example, what role does such involvement play in promoting adolescent well-being, preventing antisocial behavior (see Caldwell and Smith 2007), and establishing lifelong patterns of deep leisure satisfaction? It is possible that adolescents who pursue a form of serious leisure might serve as leisure role models for their peers, unless, of course, they are qualified as "weird" because they participate noticeably less often in casual leisure than the rest. Systematic research in this area is long overdue, but is nevertheless beginning to occur.

In other words, the SLP takes a dramatically different approach from the one usually taken in the study of crime and deviance. It explains how wayward youth and other people become attracted to amateur, hobbyist, and volunteer pursuits, rather than how they become attracted to deviance. For instance, Cardona (2010) reports that a program in Ciudad Juarez, Mexico, which helps poor children learn and play classical music has so far succeeded in keeping over 400 of them from joining the city's omnipresent drug gangs. Furthermore, the SLP helps explain the assumption on which this discussion is based, namely, that an OLL, once discovered, will prove to be so absorbing that the typical youth will find he or she has little time left for and relatively little interest in deviant activities. The empirical validity of this assumption, however, remains to be fully established by way of research (Siegenthaler and Gonsalez 1997).

On this subject, we should not expect that research will find the assumption valid for all youth. For surely there will be some who take up serious leisure *and* find time and interest to continue in or take up some sort of deviance, as well as others who will eschew every serious leisure activity suggested, preferring instead a steady diet of deviant casual leisure. Nichols (1997), for example, found in a sample of unemployed men on probation that counseling in sport sometimes fails to reduce offending. The SLP cannot explain these preferences, which are the province of the theories of crime and delinquency.

Youth and World Peace

This book has concentrated, for the most part, on the three domains of life as experienced in the Western world. Yet, some readers may wonder about the substantial part of the tumult of our time—our current personal and social problems—that originates outside the West, while still undeniably affecting it. In this respect a couple of studies show that the positive force of leisure is also at work there. One study reviews research showing that sport and recreation have been "proven" to be effective means for building peace in the Middle East (Jamieson and Ross 2007). Competition is part of sport, but so also is cooperation, team building, positive identity, group empowerment, and similar positive processes.

This is what the organizers of the Gulf Cup had in mind when they set up a two-week soccer tournament for eight Persian Gulf states, which was successfully held in Aden, Yemen, in December 2010 (Worth 2010). Yemen's government hosted the games in part to try to heal an old rift between the north and the south of the country, using casual leisure spectatorship as the vehicle for this. The healing seems to have worked, at least in the short run. There were positive feelings in both regions about the event. Even planned protest and terrorist activities never took place (security was, however, very tight). Nevertheless, as Worth observed, "the tournament has not eased the underlying grievances, and protest could resume after the national intoxication over the Gulf Cup fades."

Along different but related lines Diener and Tov (2007) studied social well-being, finding that it varies widely across nations. They observed it was associated with, among other factors, confidence in government and the armed forces, emphasis on postmaterialist values, support for democracy, and lowered intolerance of immigrants and racial groups. An elevated sense of social well-being, the authors concluded, correlates strongly with peaceful attitudes. This is clearly an important area for further research.

Conclusion

The underlying theoretic approach of this book has been Weberian. Max Weber launched his social actionist theory of society from the springboard of human interaction, with the ways people understand each other and act on the basis of that understanding. He argued that some of these interactions eventuate in interpersonal relationships, some go farther to result in groups and organizations. Culture, according to his theory, is produced by interacting people. Weber saw whole communities and societies as rooted in the interactions of their members.

Yet, it is just as possible to start theorizing about society from the standpoint of these organizational and communal structures and from the standpoint of culture to show how they influence, if not direct, human interaction. This, in broad terms, is the position taken by the structuralists and, earlier, the functionalists in the social sciences. A detailed definition of leisure created from either of these theoretic angles would have a different look from the one presented in this book. Although I know of no such definition, were one to be written, it would, compared with the definition set out in this book, very probably place much on less emphasis on agency (uncoerced activity) and much more on context. As for the scholars given to structuralist thought, part of the problem is that they have devoted rather little of it to the question of leisure (see Stebbins [2009b, 59–65], for a discussion of some of the

French thinkers in this area). So perhaps their proclivity for writing a definition of it is, at least at present, remote.

I have no intention here of wading into the long-standing debate about the role of human agency in shaping society and changing it. Obviously both the dictionary and the detailed definitions developed in this book give considerable scope to agency. I am no structuralist (or functionalist). But do I want to go on record as recognizing that other definitions are theoretically possible, and I would, in the interest of enhancing our understanding of the idea of leisure, strongly encourage contributions along these lines. In other words, this book has centered on *a* detailed definition of leisure, not *the* detailed definition. What is important is that we have one or more such statements, the number depending on however many different ways can be conceived of to define leisure.

As for the present agency-based, detailed definition, it consists in summary form, of eight unique principles. As with all my conceptual statements, in leisure studies and in other fields, I want this one to be considered exploratory. That is I have identified eight first principles, but subsequent thought and research might produce data that suggest additional principles or that challenge the validity of one or more of the original eight. Properly collected data have the last say in such matters, so we should stand prepared to rewrite this present definition when called for by the facts. The world deserves this careful attention if it is to benefit fully from the idea of leisure and experience free-time activity as progressive.

References

Aitchison, C. 2003. From leisure and disability to disability leisure: Developing data, definitions, and discourses. *Disability and Society* 18: 955–69.

Applebaum, H. 1992. *The concept of work: Ancient, medieval, and modern.* Albany, NY: State University of New York Press.

Arai, S. M., and A. M. Pedlar. 1997. Building communities through leisure: Citizen participation in a healthy communities initiative. *Journal of Leisure Research* 29: 167–82.

Barzun, J. 1956. *Music in American life.* Bloomington, IN: Indiana University Press.

Bates, M. J. 1999. The invisible substrate of information science. *Journal of the American Society for Information Science* 50, no. 12: 1043–50.

Becker, G. 1965. A theory of the allocation of time. *Economic Journal* 75: 493–517.

Belk, R. 2007. Consumption, mass consumption, and consumer culture. In *The Blackwell encyclopedia of the social sciences*, ed. G. Ritzer, 737–46. Cambridge, MA: Blackwell.

Bowen, C. D. 1935. *Friends and fiddlers.* Boston, MA: Little Brown.

Braverman, H. 1974. *Labor and monopoly capital: The degradation of work in the twentieth century.* New York: Monthly Review Press.

Brissett, D., and R. P. Snow. 1993. Boredom: Where the future isn't. *Symbolic Interaction* 16: 237–56.

Bryan, H. 1977. Leisure value systems and recreational specialization: The case of trout fishermen. *Journal of Leisure Research* 9: 174–87.

Caldwell, L, and E. Smith. 2007. Leisure as a context for youth development and delinquency prevention. In *Pathways and crime prevention: Theory, policy, and practice*, ed. A. France and R. Hommel, 271–97. Devon, UK: Willan Publishing.

Cantwell, A-M. 2003. Deviant leisure. In *Encyclopedia of leisure and outdoor recreation*, ed. J. M. Jenkins and J. J. Pigram, 114. London: Routledge.

Cardona, J. 2010. Beethoven, Bach battle Mexico gangs. *Calgary Herald*, December 7, A6 (Reuters press release).

Cohen, J. 2002. *Protestantism and capitalism: The mechanisms of influence.* New York: Aldine de Gruyter.

Cohen-Gewerc, E. 2001. Boredom, threshold of creative leisure. *Gerontology* (official journal of the Israel Gerontological Society) 30, nos. 1–2: 87–95.

Cook, D. T. 2006. Leisure and consumption. In *A handbook of leisure studies*, ed. C. Rojek, S. M. Shaw, and A. J. Veal, 304–16. New York: Palgrave Macmillan.

Cross, G. 1990. *A social history of leisure since 1600.* State College, PA: Venture.

Crouch, D. 2006. Geographies of leisure. In *A handbook of leisure studies*, ed. C. Rojek, S. M. Shaw, and A. J. Veal, 125–39. Houndmills, Basingstoke, UK: Palgrave Macmillan.

Csikszentmihalyi, M. 1990. *Flow: The psychology of optimal experience*. New York, NY: Harper & Row.

Cunningham, H. 2008. *Leisure in the industrial revolution*. London: Croom Helm.

Cushman, G., A. J. Veal, and J. Zuzanek, eds. 2005. *Free time and leisure participation: International perspectives*. Wallingford, UK: CAB International.

Davidson, L., and R. A. Stebbins. 2011. *Serious leisure and nature: Sustainable consumption in the outdoors*. Houndmills, Basingstoke, UK: Palgrave Macmillan.

Davies, M., and M. Niemann. 2002. The everyday spaces of global politics: Work, leisure, family. *New Political Science* 24: 557–77.

De Grazia, S. 1964. *Of time, work, and leisure*. Garden City, NY: Doubleday Anchor.

Delamere, F. M., and S. M. Shaw. 2006. Playing with violence: Gamers' social construction of violent video game play as tolerable deviance. *Leisure/Loisir* 30: 7–26.

Diener, E., and W. Tov. 2007. Subjective well-being and peace. *Journal of Social Issues* 63: 421–40.

Driver, B. 2003. Experiences. In *Encyclopedia of leisure and outdoor recreation*, ed. J. M. Jenkins and J. J. Pigram, 168–71. New York: Routledge.

Dubin, R. 1992. *Central life interests: Creative individualism in a complex world*. New Brunswick, NJ: Transaction.

Economist. 2005. Up off the couch. October 22, 35.

_____. 2006. The land of pleasure. February 2. http://www.Economist.com (accessed December 8, 2010).

Elkington, S. 2010. Articulating a systematic phenomenology of flow: An experience-process perspective. *Leisure/Loisir* 34: 327–60.

Frey, B. S. 2008. *Happiness: A revolution in economics*. Cambridge, MA: MIT Press.

Gelber, S. M. 1999. *Hobbies: Leisure and the culture of work in America*. New York: Columbia University Press.

Gerson, J. 2010. Video games keep kids fit. *Calgary Herald*, December 8, B1.

Gerth, H., and C. W. Mills, eds. 1958. *From Max Weber: Essays in sociology*. New York: Oxford University Press.

Getz, D. 2007. *Event studies: Theory, research and policy for planned events*. Amsterdam: Elsevier.

_____. 2008. Progress in tourism management event tourism: Definition, evolution, and research. *Tourism Management* 29: 403–28.

Gini, A. 2001. *My self, my job: Work and the creation of the modern individual*. New York: Routledge.

Godbout, J. 1990. La Participation: Instrument de Professionnalisation des Loisirs. *Loisir et Société/Society and Leisure* 9: 33–40.

Goffman, E. 1963. *Stigma: Notes on the management of spoiled identity*. Englewood Cliffs, NJ: Prentice-Hall.

Graham, M. M. 2004. Volunteering as heritage/volunteering in heritage. In *Volunteering as leisure/leisure as volunteering: An international assessment*, ed. R. A. Stebbins and M. M. Graham, 13–30. Wallingford, Oxon, UK: CAB International.

Gunn, L., and L. T. Cassie. 2006. Serial murder as an act of deviant leisure. *Leisure/Loisir* 30: 27–53.

Hamilton-Smith, E. 1993. In the Australian bush: Some reflections on serious leisure. *World Leisure & Recreation* 35, no. 1: 10–13.

Harrison, J. 2001. Thinking about tourists. *International Sociology* 16: 159–72.

Hartel, J. 2003. The serious leisure frontier in library and information science: Hobby domains. *Knowledge Organization* 30, no. 3/4: 228–38.

Heuser, L. 2005. We're not too old to play sports: The career of women lawn bowlers. *Leisure Studies* 24: 45–60.

Houle, C. O. 1961. *The inquiring mind.* Madison, WI: University of Wisconsin Press.

Huizinga, J. 1955. *Homo ludens: A study of the play element in culture.* Boston, MA: Beacon.

Hutchinson, S. L., and D. A. Kleiber. 2005. Gifts of the ordinary: Casual leisure's contributions to health and well-being. *World Leisure Journal* 47, no. 3: 2–16.

Iso-Ahola, S. E., and E. D. Crowley. 1991. Adolescent substance abuse and leisure boredom. *Journal of Leisure Research* 23: 260–71.

Jamieson, L. M., and C. M. Ross. 2007. Using recreation to curb extremism. *Parks & Recreation* 42, no. 2: 26–29.

Jarvis, P. 1995. *Adult and continuing education.* 2nd ed. London: Routledge.

Jevons, W. S. 2006. *The theory of political economy.* Boston, MA: Adamant Media Corp. (Orig. pub. 1888.)

Johnston, R. J., D. Gregory, G. Pratt, and M. Watts. 2000. *The dictionary of human geography.* 4th ed. Malden, MA: Blackwell.

Jones, I., and G. Symon. 2001. Lifelong learning as serious leisure: Policy, practice, and potential. *Leisure Studies* 20: 269–84.

Juniu, S., and K. Henderson. 2001. Problems in researching leisure and women: Global considerations. *World Leisure Journal* 43, no. 4: 3–10.

Kando, T. M., and W. C. Summers. 1971. The impact of work on leisure. *Pacific Sociological Review* 14: 313–27.

Kaplan, M. 1960. *Leisure in America: A social inquiry.* New York: John Wiley.

———. 1975. *Leisure: Theory and policy.* New York: Wiley.

Katz, J. 1988. *Seductions of crime: Moral and sensual attractions of doing evil.* New York: Basic Books.

Keen, A. 2007. *The cult of the amateur.* New York: Crown Publishing Group.

Kelly, J. R. 1990. *Leisure.* 2nd ed. Englewood Cliffs, NJ: Prentice-Hall.

———. 2000. The "real world" and the relevance of theory-based research. *Journal of Leisure Research* 32: 74–78.

Keyes, C. L. M. 1998. Social well-being. *Social Psychology Quarterly* 61: 121–40.

Kiewa, J. 2003. Consumption. In *Encyclopedia of leisure and outdoor recreation,* ed. J. M. Jenkins and J. J. Pigram, 79–91. New York: Routledge.

Killinger, B. 1997. *Workaholism: The respectable addicts.* Toronto. ON: Firefly Books.

Kleiber, D. A. 2000. The neglect of relaxation. *Journal of Leisure Research* 32: 82–86.

Lambdin, L. 1997. *Elderlearning*. Phoenix, AZ: Oryx Press.

Li, Y. n.d. Leisure study and geography of everyday life. In *Proceeding first Pacific rim conference on leisure education*, ed. N. McIntyre and H. Nishino, 7–11. (Source: http://geog.hku.hk/undergrad/geog2057/2057reference1.pdf, accessed February 22, 2010.)

Library Trends. 2009. Pleasurable pursuits: Leisure and LIS research, ed. C. Fulton and R. Vondracek, 57, no. 4: 611–768.

Machlowitz, M. 1980. *Workaholics: Living with them, working with them*. Reading, MA: Addison-Wesley.

Mannell, R. C. 1999. Leisure experience and satisfaction. In *Leisure studies: Prospects for the twenty-first century*, ed. E. L. Jackson and T. L. Burton, 235–52. State College, PA: Venture.

McBrearty, S., and C. Stringer. 2007. The coast in colour. *Nature* 449 (October 18): 793–94.

McDonald, M., S. Wearing, and J. Ponting. 2007. Narcissism and neo-liberalism: Work, leisure, and alienation in an era of consumption. *Loisir et Société/Society and Leisure* 30: 489–510.

Moss, W. G. 2008. *An age of progress? Clashing twentieth-century global forces*. New York: Anthem.

Nahrstedt, W. 2000. Global edutainment: The role of leisure education for community development. In *Leisure education, community development and populations with special needs*, ed. A. Sivan and H. Ruskin, 65–74. London: CAB International.

Nazareth, L. 2007. *The leisure economy: How changing demographics, economics, and generational attitudes will reshape our lives and our industries*. Mississauga, ON: John Wiley & Sons Canada.

Nichols, G. 1997. A consideration of why active participation in sport and leisure might reduce criminal behaviour. *Sport, Education and Society* 2: 181–90.

Oberg, L. 2008. Leisure. In *The new Palgrave dictionary of economics online*, ed. S. N. Durlauf and L. E. Blume. 2nd ed. New York: Palgrave Macmillan.

Orr, N. 2003. Heritage and leisure: Museum volunteering as "serious leisure." In *Access and inclusion in leisure and tourism*, ed. R. Snape, E. Thwaites, and C. Williams, vol. 81, 119–40. Brighton, UK: Leisure Studies Association.

Parker, S. 1983. *Leisure and work*. London: George Allen & Unwin.

Patterson, I. 2000. Developing a meaningful identity for people with disabilities through serious leisure activities. *World Leisure Journal* 42, no. 2: 41–51.

_____. 2001. Serious leisure as a positive contributor to social inclusion for people with intellectual disabilities. *World Leisure Journal* 43, no. 3: 16–24.

Pieper, J. 1952. *Leisure: The basis of culture*. New York: New American Library.

Riesman, D., N. Glazer, and R. Denney 1961. *The lonely crowd: A study of the changing American character*. rev. ed. New Haven, CT: Yale University Press.

Roberson, D. N., Jr. 2005. Leisure and learning: An investigation of older adults and self-directed learning. *Leisure/Loisir* 29: 203–38.

Roberts, K. 1999. *Leisure in contemporary society*. Wallingford, Oxon: CABI Publishing.

Robinson, J. P., and G. Godbey. 1997. *Time for life: The surprising ways Americans use their time*. University Park, PA: Pennsylvania State University Press.

Rojek, C. 1997. Leisure theory: Retrospect and prospect. *Loisir et Société/Society and Leisure* 20: 383–400.

_____. 2000. *Leisure and culture*. London: Palgrave.

_____. 2002. Civil labour, leisure and post work society. *Société et Loisir/Society and Leisure* 25: 21–36.

_____. 2005. *Leisure theory: Principles and practice*. Houndmills, Basingstoke, UK: Palgrave Macmillan.

_____. 2010. *The labour of leisure*. London: Sage.

Rosenstone, S. J., and J. M. Hansen. 1993. *Mobilization, participation, and democracy in America*. New York: Macmillan.

Samdahl, D. M. 2000. Reflections on the future of leisure studies. *Journal of Leisure Research* 32: 125–28.

Samdahl, D. M., and J. R. Kelly. 1999. Speaking only to ourselves? Citation analysis of *Journal of Leisure Research* and *Leisure Sciences*. *Journal of Leisure Research* 31: 171–80.

Scott, D. 2003. Constraints. In *Encyclopedia of leisure and outdoor recreation*, ed. J. M. Jenkins and J. J. Pigram, 75–78. London: Routledge.

Searle, M. S. 2000. Is leisure theory needed for leisure studies? *Journal of Leisure Research* 32: 138–42.

Seligman, M. E. P., and M. Csikszentmihalyi. 2000. Positive psychology: An introduction. *American Psychologist* 55, no. 1: 5–14.

Selman, G., M. Selman, M. Cooke, and P. Dampier. 1998. *The foundations of adult education in Canada*. 2nd ed. Toronto, ON: Thompson.

Shaw, S. M. 2000. If our research is relevant, why is nobody listening? *Journal of Leisure Research* 32: 147–51.

Siegenthaler, K. L., and I. O'Dell. 2003. Older golfers: Serious leisure and successful aging. *World Leisure Journal* 45, no. 1: 45–52.

Siegenthaler, K. L., and G. L. Gonsalez. 1997. Youth sports as serious leisure: A critique. *Journal of Sport and Social Issues* 21: 298–314.

Smith, D. H., R. A. Stebbins, and M. Dover. 2006. *A dictionary of nonprofit terms and concepts*. Bloomington, IN: Indiana University Press.

Sonnenberg, R. 1996. *Living with workaholism*. St. Louis, MO: Concordia Publishing House.

Spector, C. 2007. Leisure and lifelong learning: Childhood and adolescence. In *The pivotal role of leisure education: Finding personal-fulfillment in this century*, ed. E. Cohen-Gewerc and R. A. Stebbins, 71–90. State College, PA: Venture.

Statistics Canada. 2001. Caring Canadians, involved Canadians: Highlights from the 2000 national survey of giving, volunteering, and participating (cat. No. 71-542-XIE). Ottawa, ON: Ministry of Industry, Government of Canada.

Stebbins, R. A. 1979. *Amateurs: On the margin between work and leisure*. Beverly Hills, CA: Sage.

_____. 1982. Serious leisure: A conceptual statement. *Pacific Sociological Review* 25: 251–72.

_____. 1992. *Amateurs, professionals, and serious leisure*. Montreal, QC and Kingston, ON: McGill-Queen's University Press.

_____. 1994. The liberal arts hobbies: A neglected subtype of serious leisure. *Loisir et Société/Society and Leisure* 16: 173–86.

_____. 1996a. *The barbershop singer: Inside the social world of a musical hobby*. Toronto, ON: University of Toronto Press.

_____. 1996b. *Tolerable differences: Living with deviance.* 2nd ed. Toronto, ON: McGraw-Hill Ryerson. http://www.soci.ucalgary.ca/seriousleisure—Digital Library (accessed November 22, 2010).

_____. 1996c. Volunteering: A serious leisure perspective. *Nonprofit and Voluntary Action Quarterly* 25: 211–24.

_____. 1997. Casual leisure: A conceptual statement. *Leisure Studies* 16: 17–25.

_____. 1998. *After work: The search for an optimal leisure lifestyle.* Calgary, AB: Detselig.

_____. 2000a. Obligation as an aspect of leisure experience. *Journal of Leisure Research* 32: 152–55.

_____. 2000b. Optimal leisure lifestyle: Combining serious and casual leisure for personal well-being. In *Leisure and human development: Proposals for the 6th World Leisure Congress,* ed. M. C. Cabeza, 101–7. Bilbao, Spain: University of Deusto.

_____. 2001a. *New directions in the theory and research of serious leisure.* Mellen Studies in Sociology, vol. 28. Lewiston, NY: Edwin Mellen.

_____. 2001b. *Exploratory research in the social sciences.* Thousand Oaks, CA: Sage.

_____. 2001c. The costs and benefits of hedonism: Some consequences of taking casual leisure seriously. *Leisure Studies* 20: 305–9.

_____. 2001d. Volunteering—mainstream and marginal: Preserving the leisure experience. In *Volunteering in leisure: Marginal or inclusive?* ed. M. Graham and M. Foley, vol. 75, 1–10. Eastbourne, UK: Leisure Studies Association.

_____. 2002. *The organizational basis of leisure participation: A motivational exploration.* State College, PA: Venture Publishing.

_____. 2003. Boredom in free time. *Leisure Studies Association Newsletter* 64 (March): 29–31. http://www.soci.ucalgary.ca/seriousleisure—Digital Library (accessed October 3, 2010).

_____. 2004a. *Between work and leisure: The common ground of two separate worlds.* New Brunswick, NJ: Transaction.

_____. 2004b. Pleasurable aerobic activity: A type of casual leisure with salubrious implications. *World Leisure Journal* 46, no. 4: 55–58. http://www.soci.ucalgary.ca/seriousleisure —Digital Library, Other Works (accessed October 10, 2010).

_____. 2005a. Choice and experiential definitions of leisure. *Leisure Sciences* 27: 349–52.

_____. 2005b. Project-based leisure: Theoretical neglect of a common use of free time. *Leisure Studies* 24: 1–11.

_____. 2005c. *Challenging mountain nature: Risk, motive, and lifestyle in three hobbyist sports.* Calgary, AB: Detselig.

_____. 2005d. *The role of leisure in arts administration.* Occasional Paper Series, Paper No. 1. Eugene, OR: Center for Community Arts and Public Policy, University of Oregon. http://aad.uoregon.edu/icas/documents/stebbins0305.pdf (accessed December 12, 2010).

_____. 2005e. Serious leisure, recreational specialization, and complex leisure activity. *Leisure Studies Association Newsletter* 70 (March): 11–13. http://www.soci.ucalgary.ca/seriousleisure —Digital Library, "Leisure Reflections No. 8" (accessed September 16, 2010)."

_____. 2006a. Discretionary time commitment: Effects on leisure choice and lifestyle. *Leisure Studies Association Newsletter* 74 (July): 18–20. http://www. soci.ucalgary.ca/seriousleisure —Digital Library, "Leisure Reflections No. 12" (accessed November 17, 2010).

_____. 2006b. Contemplation as leisure and nonleisure. *Leisure Studies Association Newsletter* 73 (March): 21–23. http://www.soci.ucalgary.ca/ seriousleisure—Digital Library, "Leisure Reflections No. 11"(accessed October 28, 2010).

_____. 2007a. *Serious leisure: A perspective for our time.* New Brunswick, NJ: Transaction.

_____. 2007b. A leisure-based, theoretic typology of volunteers and volunteering. *Leisure Studies Association Newsletter* 78 (November): 9–12. http://www.soci. ucalgary.ca/seriousleisure —Digital Library, "Leisure Reflections No. 16"(accessed November 23, 2010).

_____. 2008a. Right leisure: Serious, casual, or project-based? *NeuroRehabilitation: An Interdisciplinary Journal* 23: 335–41.

_____. 2008b. The leisure basis of caring. *Leisure Studies Association Newsletter* 79 (March): 34–37. http://www.soci.ucalgary.ca/seriousleisure —Digital Library, "Leisure Reflections No. 17"(accessed December 1, 2010).

_____. 2009a. *Personal decisions in the public square: Beyond problem solving into a positive sociology.* New Brunswick, NJ: Transaction.

_____. 2009b. *Leisure and consumption: Common ground, separate worlds.* New York: Palgrave Macmillan.

_____. 2009c. New leisure and leisure customization. *World Leisure Journal* 51, no. 2: 78–84.

_____. 2010a. Flow in serious leisure: Nature and prevalence.*Leisure Studies Association Newsletter* 87 (November): 21–23. http://www.soci.ucalgary. ca/seriousleisure —Digital Library, "Leisure Reflections No. 25" (accessed October 9, 2010).

_____. 2010b. Fulfilling leisure for youth. *YDI research brief number 6.* AgriLife Research and Extension, Texas A&M University. http://www.ydi.tamu.edu/ briefs-and-reports (accessed September 13, 2010).

_____. 2011a. Personal memoirs, project-based leisure and therapeutic recreation for seniors. *Leisure Studies Association Newsletter* 88 (March) 29-31 http:// www.soci.ucalgary.ca/seriousleisure —Digital Library, "Leisure Reflections No. 26, " (accessed November 19, 2010).

_____. (2011b). Loisirs sérieux : un exposé conceptuel [Serious leisure : A conceptual statement]. In *Les catégories sociales et leurs frontiers* [The social categories and their boundaries], ed. C. Marry, A. Degenne, and S. Moulin, 121–46). Québec, QC: Les Presses de l'Université Laval.

Stone, G. P. 1971. American sports: Play and display. In The sociology of *sport*, ed. E. Dunning, 46–65. London: Frank Cass.

Sylvester, C. 1999. The Western idea of work and leisure: Traditions, transformations, and the future. In *Leisure studies: Prospects for the twenty-first century*, ed. E. L. Jackson and T. L. Burton, 17–34. State College, PA: Venture.

Truzzi, M. 1972. The occult revival as popular culture. *The Sociological Quarterly* 13: 16–36.

UNESCO. 1976. *Recommendation on the development of adult education.* Paris, France: UNESCO.

Unruh, D. R. 1979. Characteristics and types of participation in social worlds. *Symbolic Interaction* 2: 115–30.

_____. 1980. The nature of social worlds. *Pacific Sociological Review* 23: 271–96.

Verba, S., N. H. Nie, and J-O. Kim. 1978. *Participation and equality: A seven nation comparison.* Cambridge, UK: Cambridge University Press.

Weber, M. 1930. *The Protestant ethic and the spirit of capitalism.* Trans. T. Parsons. New York: Charles Scribners Sons.

Weiss, Y. 2009. Work and leisure: A history of ideas. *Journal of Labor Economics* 27: 1–20.

Whannel, G. 1983. *Blowing the whistle: The politics of sport.* London: Pluto Press.

Williams, R. M., Jr. 2000. American society. In *Encyclopedia of sociology*, ed. E. F. Borgatta and R. J. V. Montgomery. 2nd ed., vol. 1, 140–48. New York: Macmillan.

Witt, P. A. 2000. Leisure research is to matter II. *Journal of Leisure Research* 32: 186–89.

Worth, R. F. 2010. Yemen loses in soccer, but scores a p.r. victory. *New York Times*, December 6 (online edition).

Yoder, D. G. 1997. A model for commodity intensive serious leisure. *Journal of Leisure Research* 29: 407–29.

Index